THE SOUNDING SYMBOL
Music Education in Action

George Odam

Stanley Thornes (Publishers) Ltd

© George Odam 1995

First published in 1995 by
Stanley Thornes (Publishers) Ltd
Ellenborough House
Wellington Street
Cheltenham
Glos. GL50 1YD
UK

ISBN 0 7487 2323 4

Typeset by Northern Phototypesetting Co Ltd, Bolton
Printed in Great Britain by The Bath Press, Avon

CONTENTS

To Jack Dobbs, with gratitude

Acknowledgements

Every effort has been made to contact copyright holders, and we apologise if any have been overlooked.

INTRODUCTION

Over the years my classroom observations of students in initial training and of teachers in service have focused increasingly on how teachers can most enhance real musical experience for their pupils in the classroom, the seminar room and the instrumental studio. Somehow the very act of teaching can seem to push real musical experience into the background. Too often the symbols we use appear to get in the way of sounds they represent; sometimes they replace them altogether. Real musical experience engages both cognitive perception and feeling response, and involves the participant at a deep personal level. It happens when conditions are right and cannot be totally assured by planning. Its first condition is that music must be heard; the second is that those involved in making or listening to it, or both, must be willing to be captured by the experience. They do not come to it. It comes to them. Real musical experience involves us fully in thinking and feeling and is, in effect, a form of spiritual experience.

In this book I want to explore some of the evidence about how we approach and learn about music and to encourage in some readers an increasingly wider net of related thoughts about music education. Most particularly I want to examine two issues: the way teachers deal with sound and its symbolization and how we best provide real musical experience for our pupils. Having taught and watched teachers and trainees working for many years I have become concerned by the way that reliance on the decoding of symbols – reading music notation – has become a sticking point with teachers and also proves a disincentive to many pupils. Often I have felt that the direct teaching of notation has been in opposition to the provision of real musical experience. Somehow these two issues are caught up together.

Learning from other cultures

Since my early training under Jack Dobbs's inspiring tutorage at the Institute of Education in London, I have been strongly affected and concerned by the difference in attitude towards fundamental musical learning in our Western European society in contrast with that of other societies in different areas of the world. There is a built-in problem in the approach our society takes to education which fundamentally affects music education and is, in my opinion, holding back what should be an enormous forward leap following the National Curriculum decisions of recent years.

Most other cultures base their education of musicians on aural tradition, many of them never finding it relevant or necessary to write down their procedures. Aural memory is capitalized from the earliest age through imitation and development of technique and there is no strongly defined role-difference between performer and composer. This places real musical experience right in the centre of things. In line with all other subjects, music education is deeply affected by our Western emphasis on linear logic, our need to write everything down and to rely for much of our information on the written word or notation. This book is an example. Western European approaches to music education declare an intention of making aural experience central, but become so caught up in the semantics, history, logics and symbols for music that the development of an acutely sensitive aural perception is not always given pride of place.

Observance of subject borders and task specification lead us in the West to separate performers from composers, reducing the ability of musicians to improvise and producing students who, while they are willing to re-create the music of others unquestioningly, will not take musical decisions for themselves. Often teachers complain that their pupils, when performing, just do not listen well enough, and this suggests that the education system through which those pupils have come has somehow encouraged them to separate out the two areas of listening and performing as discrete disciplines.

Why do we do what we do?

Much of the good practice inherent in the British National Curriculum advice documents and guidelines will not flower from well-rooted music education stock if teachers continue to teach music without careful consideration of this central problem of lack of musical experience. A solution cannot be achieved merely through seeing what works; there must be some enquiry into why it is that we do what we do. This book is an attempt to begin to find some of the essential questions, even if no firm answers are yet forthcoming.

As well as being strongly and positively affected by the excellent philosophy texts of Bennett Reimer and Keith Swanwick and the inspiring work John Paynter has done, I have found other strong pointers towards a solution through enquiry into the biological and psychological factors that underlie our actions – by learning from some basic principles which govern the way that the brain receives and processes music.

Over the last last three decades there has been a considerable amount of scientific research into this. John Sloboda's cognitive psychology text (*The Musical Mind*, 1985) and David Hargreaves's work in developmental psychology (*The Developmental Psychology of Music*, 1986) are illuminating about the way learning takes place but do not look in any detail at its application in teaching. New medical evidence using topographical brain mapping is currently producing revealing and far-reaching evidence of the listening process. Psychology has been underplayed in initial and continuing teacher education now for many years, giving preference to the pragmatic approach. My years of teacher education have been dedicated to the practical and the pragmatic, but I feel that it is important now to make certain that we do not simply ignore what science is telling us about brain function for dogmatic reasons. After an enquiry into the way we use symbols and treat music as a quasi-language in Chapter 1, Chapter 2 will attempt to summarize those central scientific matters concerning the way in which we perceive music, based on accredited work of biologists and neuropsychologists that is reasonably uncontentious and from which we, as music teachers, can learn much. The following chapters attempt to describe music education in action, adding reflective comment in the light of this information.

I am aware that this whole area of scientific research and application to music education is, for some music educators, like a red rag to a bull. Somehow a very deep prejudice has been built up in this country against any kind of link between how musicians think and brain research. The mystery of art appears to them to be assaulted, and the myriad complexities of the brain reduced to a mere simplistic compartmentalizing of areas. I have been fascinated, however, to observe such research as it has gradually been fed through over the last thirty years in articles and a few books, and to note how clearly there is a resonance between the problems of integrating sounds and their musical symbols and brain laterality and whole-brain thinking (in as much as we understand it at present). Interestingly, as new and sophisticated computer-driven techniques of enquiry are brought into play, the resonances become stronger, enlightening even more clearly the central problem of music teaching that lacks essential musicality. Partly, this can be ascribed to the way in which, unquestioningly, we tend to treat music as a language. This is the first problem I want to address in Chapter 1.

Structure

I have chosen to set out my text in an unusual manner. Each of the eight chapters has a common structure. First is given the basic text, followed, not that unusually, by a resumé of the main issues from that chapter. After this is a new section called "Teaching implications", and in this I have tried to provide practical examples to follow up aspects of the theory into practice in the classroom. There are examples from a variety of teaching situations, from early years to higher education and instrumental teaching. Wherever or with whomsoever teachers pursue music education, my perception is that there are common principles that guide good practice.

THE SOUNDING SYMBOL

Music as "language"

In contrast to the imperfection of verbal thought, which painfully encounters its own limits, language being insufficient ("If one cannot say a thing, one must be silent about it": Wittgenstein), musical thought is constructed exclusively on its own material, not upon an abstraction lying outside the discipline, but upon the supply of musical tones, infinitely enriched by timbres. It formulates with the greatest possible differentiation and precision. But what does it formulate? ... Music has at least as definite a meaning as words, although it cannot be translated into words (Mendelssohn).

Hildesheimer (1977).

The problem I wish to identify, that of lack of emphasis on real musical experience in the practice of music education, is focused a great deal in our use of and attitude towards language, most particularly on what is written down, and this includes music notation. Somehow this reliance on the written fundamentally affects our willingness to trust in and develop our aural memory. It can lead to an attitude towards music that gives preference to concrete meaning and pays little attention to overall metaphoric and analogous relationships. Since a performing musician's concentration tends to be on the exact interpretation of the surface detail of music, it can often become difficult, as it were, to see the wood for the trees. But understanding music as metaphor, or identifying in music those procedures that have clear analogies with other life areas, can help musicians to place their art alongside other arts and to begin to perceive connections between them.

The understanding of metaphor in brain terms is fundamentally opposed to the understanding of language and linear logic, and this will be better explained in Chapter 2. But the brain can integrate both of these kinds of understanding, like a hidden stereoscopic image, producing a new image in a new dimension. We have, through experience and, one hopes, through education, to learn to enliven and control these two opposed areas, and it needs some practice. All artists, musicians included, need to learn to develop their appreciation of metaphoric relationships and to stimulate that intuitive part of our thinking process which appreciates them just as much as that which prefers the computational and linear. On the whole, traditional Western music education strengthens the latter at the expense of the former.

It is impossible to read much about music or talk about it with interested people without coming across the notion that music actually is a language. It is a commonly held, perhaps central, metaphor. Much has been written on this over the last forty years, in particular the well-known book *The Language of Music* by Deryck Cooke (1959), the philosophic writings of Suzanne Langer (1951) and the musicological texts of L. B. Meyer (1956, 1967). In the late 1970s Hans Keller, in a

Wittgenstein notes that we may be very familiar with a favourite piece, say a Haydn Minuet, and yet want to hear it again – want to hear specifically that piece and not another one similar to it. Wittgenstein asks why we should want to hear just that piece. After all, it holds no surprises for us. Here we suggest that although it may hold no surprises for us on the conscious level, it is full of schematic violations on the subconscious level. Now of course it would be possible to listen to it so often (several dozen times consecutively for example) that we would habituate even these subconscious responses to it. That is, our schemata for the type of piece and the style would simply come to mirror this particular piece as a prototype. ... If the meaning of music were entirely accessible at explicit verbal levels, we would not actually have to listen to it – we could just talk about it. ... words name things, but music does not name. Rather it conveys meaning in the relationship among signs embodied in a complex semiotic system.

Dowling and Harwood (1986).

No one any longer asserts that music is an "absolute world of tones and sonorities". But neither can anyone explain the paradox that it is, on the one hand, transitory in its performance, but also "something eternal" in its continuity, a treasure store that is immediate to us only when it is presented again and again. Be that as it may, today we have to think of music as an important medium of communication. But the information, the partnership between the informant and the informed, escapes both analysis and calculation, because it conveys no semantic meaning. It cannot be translated into words, but exists and functions parallel to them, as a supplementary and yet fully fledged means of expression. This is true, of course, only for absolute music, that is, music without extra-musical content. It comes to us as a stimulus; as such it mobilizes feelings that are reserved exclusively for it and is assimilated according to the receptivity of the listener. We exchange our feelings, compare our associations, and from the result conclude something *a posteriori* about the possible "situation" (*Befindlichkeit*) (Heidegger's "translation" of the word "mood" (*Stimmung*) which seems useful to me here) of the creator.

Hildesheimer (1977).

memorable set lecture on the subject, summarized the position with typical clarity and wit. His central point hinged on the lack of any dictionary which spells out what this so-called language really means, despite Cooke's persuasive arguments. The terminology commonly used to describe Cooke's focus on the expressive function of musical intervals is "designative meaning". Sloboda (1985) analyses this issue in great detail. Designative meaning, he explains, is that which refers outside the music to objects or events in the non-musical domain. Reimer (1970, 2/1989) uses the term "referential meaning" for the same phenomenon. The more we treat music like a language, the more important the written notation of music becomes in the study of it as we increasingly seek for certain forms of meaning.

Historically, music education has preferred to explore embodied meaning, which is that which we understand and feel from knowing about, and making predictions about, the actual substance and structure of the music itself. It is language-based, and this search for embodied meaning can easily be enhanced through studying notation. The search for embodied meaning can lead to learning which concentrates on technique as an end in itself, increasingly ignoring both the world of ideas and aesthetics and that of sound. It can also encourage a kind of "check-list" attitude to music that does not engage with feelings or meanings below the surface. At its worst it can treat the actual sound as a sort of optional extra, relying on verbal descriptions of sound or notational equivalents. Formal analysis teachers in higher education sometimes find that the use of sound in their sessions merely holds things up. The intricacies of harmonic frameworks, set analysis, invariants as compositional determinants and so on soon take the place of sound and become separately intriguing.

"Good-enough" music teachers need to be aware when they are using music as a quasi-language and when they are not. In other words they should be sure when they are engaging in designative meaning and when in embodied meaning. Both forms have their tale to tell. Such teachers need particularly to be able to engage their students in the world of ideas and to create in them a feeling of ownership for their own programmes of study. At the same time they need to create excitement in using and respect for the actual substance and structure. It is the exchange between designative and embodied meaning within teaching that can bring about the richest form of synthesis and provide the best basis for such an aim. As in most things, finding the balance is all, and to find the balance you need to know where the weight is.

Music as metaphor

"The linguistic analogy", Sloboda (1985) says, "is neither true nor false. Like all analogies, it achieves a partial fit with its subject." I would wish to push the argument a little further in observing that analogies, or metaphors, don't function if they do fit. If they fit they cease to become analogies and become, rather, descriptions. It is in the tension between fit and non-fit that their power lies. Their function is to exist as a certain form of truth in conveying meaning alongside other forms of meaning whose function is always to "fit". Musical thinking and experience draw as much upon metaphor as they do upon rational analysis. To be able to progress successfully in anything we have to be able to synthesize both of these areas of thought, the metaphoric and the logical, through some form of action which acts as a mediator between these two incompatible areas. My position throughout this book is that such synthesis is paramount. It is what is fashionably labelled "holistic".

My book's title, "The Sounding Symbol", as well as punning on the word "cymbal", plays with the words and symbols of a well-known quotation and arrives at a combination which in terms of normal language doesn't make conventional sense or appears to be non-syntactical. In violating the original expectation I have provided a surprise – a new combination and new resonance. One of the distinguishing features of the artistic is being able to provide surprising new combinations of previously disparate things. Our logical brain considers the combination and accepts or rejects the proposition. The question it must ask itself in this case is "do symbols sound?" A first answer might be that symbols, which are mainly the province of the eye, do not sound. A further consideration might produce the thought, "but if you speak the word or give the pictograph a name then it does make a sound."

Making musical symbols sound so clearly in the memory that they can be converted to appropriate live sound when required is a central task of good music education. In this manipulation of sense and image, logic and sideways thinking, I am putting forward a central metaphor referring to the core problem of music teaching, that of stimulating opposing areas of thinking and feeling and integrating them into a new whole: making symbols sound.

Symbols and sounds

As music has developed in the Western world it has evolved a variety of systems of symbols for sounds whose function it is to record accurately.

The evolution of both the art of music and its notation has been mutually interdependent. The easier it was to record musical thoughts and structures, the longer or more complex the music could be. In early times, Western musicians relied solely on their aural memories to preserve the music they invented or learnt. As the use of notation grew and it became readily available in printed form, musicians relied on it increasingly for the complete storage and retrieval of music, no longer finding it necessary to memorize. Most parameters of the music are stored in Western notation, leaving only a small area for personal interpretation.

In our society, however, a considerable proportion of practising musicians exist, and have always existed, who only occasionally need or use music notation. For them, the sound stored well in the head does not require such a complex written record. Where it has been necessary to write something down, general labelling and simple graphic symbol systems have evolved and are still in common use. Their use depended, and still does depend, on a keen aural memory of the style and type of music to be played. Since the function of such labels and symbols is largely mnemonic, much is left to individual decision. Aurally based musicians are concerned principally with manipulation of the sound

Though I speak with the tongues of men and of angels, and have not charity, I am become as a sounding brass, or a tinkling cymbal.

I Corinthians 13:1

Surprise is the privilege only of prepared minds – it takes preparation to discern what is trivially improbability and what is effective surprise.

Bruner, J. S. (1967). The Conditions of Creativity in Contemporary Approaches to Creative Thinking. New York: Atherton Press.

Trained musicians tend to regard music as an ongoing series of interrelated events over longer periods of time ... This perception requires short- and long-term memory, internal perceptual representations, and strategies of temporal organization similar to that we observe in motor skills or verbal syntax. When this in-depth analysis is required, the evidence indicates that trained musicians tend to process music with their dominant hemisphere ...

Thus, it is plausible to hypothesize that in the process of learning musical tasks that involve sequential programmes, analogous to most of language, speech or praxis, there would be an initial tendency to share specialized neural processors with most of the other functions. Thus, the preferential left hemisphere *lateralization* found in musicians would be due both to the cognitive "linguistic" structure of classical music, the need for *their* processing along *syntactical algorhythms* and in general to cognitive operations that imply related computations and prelearned internal representations.

Martin (1982).

A child's perception of the visual may be confused by equating visual understanding to verbal literacy, or the written word. "Art criticism" delivered inappropriately may not encourage a personal "making" response to the visual arts. It could be that the National Curriculum guidelines for Art Education, which encourage "discussing" the visual arts, may be responsible for discouraging "making" and "responding" to the visual world in a way that is different from talking and writing.

Charlton, J. (1994). The Potency of the Narrative Image. Exeter University: unpubd dissertation.

… The interruptions afforded by music are not often materially frustrating, and composers search for satisfying resolutions. Thus music serves as a marvellous cultural invention for providing positive emotional experiences in a more or less unsatisfying world.

… Concerning symbols, we invoked Mandler's theory of emotion to describe the way emotional experience can arise out of stylistically embedded expectancies.

Dowling and Harwood (1986).

itself, but those who rely upon notation must concern themselves with interpreting the symbol.

Our music education system is biased towards the practice of the latter group of notation users, yet the larger number of pupils we teach aspires to the former. The best practice in music education takes the virtues of both approaches; we need to strengthen the aural memories of notation readers and to encourage less dependence on notation, and aurally reliant pupils need to discover the benefits of the skill of reading. This study is not centred on notation as such, but I have come to see, in the way in which we make use of notation, a central problem for all music teachers that derives from a need to strengthen our musical memories and, ultimately, from the way we approach musical learning.

The more we rely upon symbol systems, the more important education processes become. Thinking in sound, imagining sound, constructing possible sounds in the head and improvising music all have to be established as skills before the symbols for these things are learnt. When we eventually use the symbols we have already to know how they will sound.

I am keenly aware of the benefits inherent in learning to read and use notation and I consider access to notation to be a key issue of music education policy. Reading and writing music is empowering; it also has its dangers. In exploring how we best teach about the sound as well as the symbol, I will try to focus on the detail of what a teacher actually does, identifying some of the features of what I consider to be good practice. I will also attempt to synthesize from them some of the guiding principles of delivery which best bring real musical experience to pupils. By the term "delivery" I mean those things the teacher actually does in the classroom to bring the curriculum to life.

Music in the curriculum

The years from 1990 to 1994 have proved to be milestone years in the development of music education in Great Britain. The decision to include music as a foundation subject in a statutory National Curriculum has provided a concentration of thought and action in music education theory and practice. Many documents have been prepared for public debate and have been subject to intensive enquiry from many sections of society. Through general consultation on the National Curriculum, music has raised considerably more positive public reaction than was expected by the government, and this has given a real boost to music's place in the curriculum at a time when "rationalization" means cutting out whatever is considered superfluous by ministers, governors and senior management teams. The arts can too easily appear superfluous to many of those in power.

There are powerful arguments against the central dictation of the school curriculum since it militates against the individuality of teachers' ideas and imposes values and systems on them about which they have no choice. This is inevitably, of course, what teachers do to children, with or without a National Curriculum. On the other hand one can view an individualistic system as too loose and anarchic,

open to abuse and only working well in the hands of inspiring teachers. For better or worse, Britain has chosen to set out a statutory National Curriculum, and that it actually includes music at all can be seen to be something of a miracle. Its exclusion from a statutory curriculum would have been disastrous. The documents for music have come out clearly in favour of an analysis of that structure of the music education curriculum articulated in the work of Bennett Reimer (*A Philosophy of Music Education*) and, most importantly, Keith Swanwick (*A Basis for Music Education* and *Music, Mind and Education*). They have taken over Swanwick's proposition of a tripartite programme based on listening (*audition* in his terminology), composing (*inventing* in Scottish terminology) and performing, assisted by literary knowledge and executant skill development. Compared with the much more prescriptive curriculum plans in England and Wales proposed for core subjects such as mathematics and English, where a fierce debate has ensued over a prescribed canon of literature and the teaching of grammar, music has been provided with a flexible enough model. Both music and art operate through guidelines rather than prescriptive programmes, and the slimmed down versions of both, produced after only two years' trial, have offered teachers considerable room for freedom of action. The immediate result in those British schools governed by the National Curriculum has been that they plan in some detail for music education. The short-term effect has been in the considerable up-grading of interest in and commitment to music education in the classroom, especially in primary schools. Its long-term success will depend on how much teachers are prepared to make the system their own and to find ways within the operation of the guidelines to express their own feelings and priorities.

Teaching the curriculum

The experience of teachers who have had little or no formal training in music education is that music is difficult to teach, particularly at ages seven to eleven. (In English and Welsh government terminology this is known as Key Stage 2 – ages five to seven being Key Stage 1, 11 to 14 Key Stage 3 and 14 to 16 Key Stage 4. For convenience I will adopt this terminology throughout the book, although I am keenly aware of the differing jargon in other parts of the British Isles, and the implications use of such jargon carries.)

The most prevalent reason given for this insecurity about teaching music is that the challenge to the teachers' personal skills is too great and exposing, since the model of music education for most adults has been of the teacher playing an instrument, singing and leading the group. This can be a great disincentive to many teachers, although modern resources are beginning to provide new support.

A more insidious and fundamental problem lies in the way that most of us actually perceive music. For the majority, a musical experience is taken in through appreciation of overall shape and contour, pulse and pattern and is enjoyed in a very general and unenquiring way. As we listen we are free to form images or metaphors which are personal and our feelings can be affected. Listening to music for structure, sequential thought, logics and predictions, for instance, requires a differently

Man uses the spoken or written word to express the meaning of what he wants to convey. His language is full of symbols, but he also often employs signs or images that are not strictly descriptive. Some are mere abbreviations or strings of initials, such as UN, UNICEF, or UNESCO; others are familiar trade marks, the names of patent medicines, badges, or insignia. Although these are meaningless in themselves, they have acquired a recognizable meaning through common usage or deliberate intent. Such things are not symbols. They are signs, and they do no more than denote the objects to which they are attached.

What we call a symbol is a term, a name, or even a picture that may be familiar in daily life, yet that possesses specific connotations in addition to its conventional and obvious meaning. It implies something vague, unknown, or hidden from us.

Thus a word or an image is symbolic when it implies something more than its obvious and immediate meaning. It has a wider "unconscious" aspect that is never precisely defined or fully explained. Nor can one hope to define it or explain it. As the mind explores the symbol, it is led to ideas that lie beyond the grasp of reason.

Jung, C. G. (1990). Man & His Symbols. Harmondsworth: Arkana.

Notation and Nomenclature.
The methods of writing down music so that it can be performed. These are devices for which the human being long felt no need, and although every race has its music, they are still unknown to the larger part of the world's population. They are apparently purely European in origin and even in Europe thousands of tunes existed which were transmitted by one generation to another without being recorded on paper until the folk-song collectors came on the scene. The plainsong of the Church also must have been communicated orally in earlier centuries.

Kennedy, M. (1980). Concise Oxford Dictionary of Music. Oxford: Oxford University Press.

An index represents its referent by having been associated with it in the past, as lightning and thunder with a storm. An icon represents through formal similarity to the referent, as a wiring diagram represents a circuit. Symbols represent by being embedded in a formal system such as a language … Indexical representation involves the emotions previously associated with the extramusical object coming to be associated with the music …

With iconic representation we turn to effects that depend upon patterns within the music itself. Music can represent the emotions iconically because the ebb and flow of tensions and relaxations in the music mirror the form of emotional tensions and relaxations

Dowling and Harwood (1986).

concentrated mental set, and many people have simply never experienced this. Similarly, many get a peripheral pleasure from looking at paintings or sculptures and reading or listening to poetry and drama without ever having "enquired within". I hope to show how this problem in perception is linked with the way our society demands use of certain mental skills and accentuates particular types of perceptions and understandings while underplaying, or even dismissing, others. As teachers, we need to be aware how much this is reflected in our actual biological make-up and in the methods society has evolved to equip us with life-skills.

Curriculum development in all subject areas has focused strongly on the key issue of strategic planning, and this has been heightened for us by the introduction of the National Curriculum. In the past, planning for music in schools was never a strong point, particularly in those schools for older children where specialists relied heavily on public examination syllabuses for overall structure – if, indeed, such structure existed. Far too many of our secondary schools had no music education syllabus, and the lack of such a syllabus was sometimes even seen as a matter of pride. Primary schools have suffered for decades from a severe lack of expertise, and there are still many around the country where a whole school staff lacks any real specialism or experience in music. In-service support is at best sporadic, and diminishing in the face of local government reforms.

Planning for music education is now a priority for all primary school class-based teachers as well as for specialists at all levels, and examples of good practice are beginning to emerge in many parts of the country. For several years new music education support materials for use in schools have become readily available. Alongside *Silver Burdett Music* (1989) have appeared such publications as *Music File* (1988–95), *Music Matters* (1992), *Growing Up With Music* (1992), the WOMAD Foundation's *Exploring the Music of the World* (1993) and many others. Considered together with the extensive advice documents published by the government authorities in England, Wales, Scotland and Northern Ireland there has never been such a wealth of available ideas and plans for the subject. Practical books and information packs have been arriving both from publishers and from regional and county authorities on planning the music curriculum, and these are aiding the establishment of good practice in a great many schools. Despite this, there appears still to be a large problem in putting such advice and information into effective practice in the classroom.

There is a commonly held opinion that music education is the province only of schools. My contention is that it takes place whenever a person endeavours to explain or reveal some new aspect of music to someone else. Music education is not simply the business of schools and teachers. It is the business of parents who wish to introduce their children to music, of instrumentalists who teach others to play and who play to other people, of composers who write music for others – most particularly music for those of us who are modest in our skill. It is the business of composers who teach others to compose, of lecturers, tutors and professors of music and music education, of those who work as musicians in our communities and of those who train others for a lifetime of working with music in some aspect.

I have never found the job of teaching music basically very different, whether I am teaching children in an infant class, a junior class, a secondary class or in higher and continuing education. The same principles apply, although the language, articulation, speed of delivery, tone of voice, facial and body language and all those things which go to make up communication skills do vary. It is those basic motivating structural principles which lie beneath the "wrapping" that I will attempt to identify in this book.

Resumé

- When we treat music like a language we can become ensnared in linear and logical thinking processes appropriate to the understanding of language but antipathetic to the achievement of musical experience. By drawing upon both metaphoric and logical thought processes through action, music provides an essential activity for the development of the brain. Language functions differently from music. Teachers need to understand this and to balance approaches to embodied meaning and designative meaning to help to provide access to musical meaning and experience.

- The evolution of symbols for sound typifies the development of Western music. How we can imagine that sound in our head, and how symbols can stand for those sounds, are crucial matters in Western music education. The provision of real musical experience through music education is the most important focus for teachers.

- Music education is not confined to the school curriculum. Its principles cover pre-school, further and higher education and all instrumental teaching, and they are equally affected by the same fundamental matters.

- After generations of random neglect, music is now a statutory subject in all schools and considerable public support has been shown for music education via the national consultation process. The quality of music education has been enhanced by curricular statements based on good principles of leading music educators.

- Effective delivery in the classroom is rooted in strong strategic planning, but many teachers, lacking good music education in their own formative years, have problems in the perception of music and of identifying and understanding its procedures. Music lessons often lack real musical experience which engages cognitive and affective responses in synthesis. Lack of real musical experience in our classrooms puts the new curriculum strategy at risk.

Teaching implications

In teaching a song or a movement activity, listening to music with pupils, directing their performance, teaching them to play an instrument, analysing a score, it is too easy to initiate the activity and to ignore the musical impulse which lies at its heart. The song can be taught for the words only; the movement activity can use music peripherally as a background; listening can be simply a passive act while the pupils are engaged in something else such as writing or drawing; performing can be concerned merely with the doing process;

In order to make up our minds we must know how to feel about things; and to know how we feel about things we need the public images of sentiment that only ritual, myth, and art can provide.

Geertz, C. (1975). The Interpretation of Cultures. London: Hutchinson.

One area to be tackled ... is the "fear and trepidation" of the generalist teacher who, when faced with taking a class of 10 or 11 year olds for music, often thinks: "This is too specialist for me."

Martin, B. (1994). "Building bridges": Yamaha educational supplement, 18 Coda, summer.

instrumental teaching can be focused solely on technical matters and analysis on the shapes and logics of the notation only. In doing all this we can bypass real musical experience, since in every case the main focus of the learning is not in the sound of the music which is at the heart of the musical experience.

It is important to plan lessons, taking into account what we know about how we receive and process music. But despite all our best planning, learning is such an unpredictable thing that we have to be prepared for a moment of revelation to take place without our having planned it and to go with it when it does. Moments of revelation occur when the class and teacher are caught up by the power of the music and stem from actual experience of the sound of music. Lesson planning over both long and short term is essential, as is syllabus design, but teachers have also to know when they can be drawn away from it. Planning must aim for a high exposure to musical sound.

Teachers should consider how much talk there is in their teaching and whether it gets in the way of the musical experience, and how much opportunity there is for music to be heard and to be repeated. They should examine the balance between the two and allow the musical experience to dominate.

Musical experience requires focused attention from those encountering it. Teachers must provide the focus and act as knowledgeable guides. In providing such a focus, they should consider how many other forms of communication can be used that are not verbal. They should consider also how much of a lesson can be taught without actually saying anything or using written language. How much they could use shape, line, texture and colour, and how much they can draw parallels with other arts and help to increase students' sensitivity to them should be matters of concern. They should also think whether they could play or sing a lesson; be concerned about how visually stimulating is the environment provided for the students and how this might enhance musical learning, or consider how often it should change.

In questioning pupils teachers should use those questions which stimulate holistic macro-thinking – questions which have many alternative answers – and those which ask "What if"? They must ask themselves how much they can balance these questions with those alternatives that stimulate detailed thinking, logical detail, sequenced thought and verbal reasoning.

Brain, Body, Music

2

Thinking, feeling, doing

This chapter provides perhaps the biggest challenge to the reader and is concerned with a central principle: that of getting the most from our brain, particularly in a musical context. If we are going to maximize the use of our brain in any task, whether musical or not, we need to find out how to get the best from it by trying to understand some of the processes and devices it employs to enable us to think, feel and do. Teachers need to be aware of how children learn in order to aid such development. Children also need to be aware of the potential their brain has and how best to enhance it.

Most of us are used to making the distinction in our daily lives between thinking and feeling. We constantly make decisions and act upon them and we may be aware that the processes which guide our actions are not always the same. A common experience is, "Well, I *think* it should be right but it just doesn't *feel* right." We can spend hours of our time analysing and assessing a complex task where choice has to be made only to find that our final decision is taken through what we call a "gut reaction".

This duality of thinking and feeling, at the heart of the brain process, must be of concern to teachers, especially to those who teach in the arts, where feeling is as important as thinking. Western European education gives a great deal of priority to thinking processes and teachers are most used to strategies that promote such activity. Although we can all be aware of this duality, we also know that we do not function in such a separate way. However, we are often far too unaware of the way in which we, as individuals, use and choose opposing brain functions and integrate them. Music education must be equally concerned in stimulating both the feeling process and the thinking process and in integrating them fully.

Many of our daily tasks are guided by actions which we have learnt but which we do not think about very much. Certain of them, breathing for instance, we have never consciously had to learn, unless in later life we suffer some respiratory problems and have to think consciously about how we do it; if we learn to sing or to play an instrument we have to learn how to build upon and extend what we have instinctively. Some actions, like walking, have to be learnt very early in life. Some modes of behaviour, driving for example, are learnt in adult life but soon become what we colloquially call "second nature". It is obvious that we draw upon different forms of storage, retrieval and motivation in all our thinking, feeling and doing. Those three areas, thinking, feeling and doing, also have a variety of different forms, and these human experiences are initiated, controlled and monitored by our brain, whose structure has evolved to promote our three basic functions.

The Buddhist and Taoist concept of the Yin and Yang and the Classical Greek division of experience into Apollonian or Dyonisian both acknowledge two fundamentals, those of thinking and feeling. Teachings which arise from these ancient philosophies also emphasize the human ability to make appropriate choices between two opposites. The secret of healthy life, they suggest, is to be found in the balancing of these opposites. The same acknowledgement of duality is to be found worldwide at the heart of the work of many poets, artists and writers and has an important central role in the work of philosophers and psychologists.

It is concluded that with a careful choice of music and its mode of presentation, one can intentionally either impede or maximize learning of tasks having known hemispheric lateralization.

McFarland, R. and Kennison, R. (1988). "Asymmetrical effects of music upon spatial-sequential learning", California State University Journal of General Psychology, 115, July.

Corpus callosum: It has been known for a long time that the minds of infants are not differentiated. Their minds, not yet affected by the culture in which they live, are almost totally metaphoric. Furthermore, the corpus callosum is not yet constricted, and the two hemispheres are nearly mutually blended together in a single brain. As growth takes place and the brain increases in size, the relative size of the connecting linkages seems to decrease. This may just be the effect of both hemispheres growing on both sides of a conduit that remains the same size as it was in infancy. However, not only does the size of the connecting linkages seem to change, but so too does their quality. They appear to get more compressed, firmer, and the smooth "open window" connection becomes a fibrous filter between the minds. This seems to happen at some time between three and four years old. The metaphoric mind is the mind of an infant, the split brain and logic/linear brain arises from it at a later stage.

Samples (1976).

Some of the most exciting biological research of this century has been in exploring the working structures of the brain. Although such research is still in its early stage, we are privileged to understand far more about how better to approach using our brains than at any time in history. Such information, despite its tentative first conclusions, should not be ignored by any teachers. Music educators can draw particular benefit from it since the pursuit of musical learning involves so many areas of the brain working in close cooperation.

Our flexible friend

An important thing to understand about the working of our brain is that it is infinitely adaptable and flexible and will alter its own processes according to the task given it. Just like other vital body structures, the younger it is, the more flexible it is and the more able to adapt. The outcome of a task will vary according to which part of the brain is given that task. We are able to choose which part of the brain we use or which areas we use in combination, although most people are not really aware of this possibility of choice and do not use it to their advantage. In learning to make such choices, we become increasingly efficient at achieving our goals. The less we are aware of our ability to choose and use appropriate brain functions, the less well we function and the more we are in danger of chaotic thinking, depression and irrational action. One of the most important functions of a teacher is to help pupils to identify how and when to use what processes, and most particularly how to make them function together in mental and physical harmony.

Music educators, like all other teachers, will find themselves promoting verbal reasoning and logical thought processes in the tasks they set their pupils, whereas the same tasks may well be able to be differently fulfilled through, for instance, the use of aural and spatial perception and contour identification. Learning to engage and to encourage the use of alternative strategies, bringing appropriate brain processes to the task, is at the heart of all good teaching.

A layman's guide to brain structure

In simple terms the brain is divided into two roughly equal hemispheres. The point of laterality runs from the nose, over the head and down to the back of the neck. The two equal hemispheres to the left and right of the point of laterality interrelate through a joining device called the "corpus callosum", a wide band of nerve fibres which facilitates contact and interaction. The corpus callosum does not reach its fullest operational state until a child attains puberty.

The actual mechanism of the corpus callosum is still a bit of a mystery and there is some evidence to suggest that there may be slight gender differences in structure. The flow of information backwards and forwards between the two hemispheres and across the corpus callosum is an essential part of good learning. We need both hemispheres to be able to live our lives fully. Each hemisphere has its assigned tasks, and we can benefit by learning what they are and how we can enhance their functioning.

The bi-hemispheral brain, which provides human beings with unique features not to be found in other animals, has evolved specialized tasks which establish themselves in the early years of life. One of the hemispheres, because it contains within it the vital skills of speech, mathematical calculation, storing of factual information and logical analysis, has become more dominant in function. This left hemisphere is objective in its approach and can help us form important concepts such as knowing how effective we are being and how well we are.

The other hemisphere contains complementary powers of comprehension of analogy and metaphor, tonal and timbral sound, shape, orientation, spatial awareness and responsiveness to colour and the diverse meanings of words. The right hemisphere processes musical pitch recognition. It is specialized in synthesis as opposed to analysis. The thinking processes here are subjective and tell us how we feel and how we relate to things and other people. It is important to stress that both sides of the brain "think", but the form or mode of cognition in the left hemisphere is fundamentally and complementarily different from that of the right. The tendency for medical writers and researchers to name the left hemisphere "dominant" or "major" and the right "non-dominant" or "minor" is more socially than neurologically determined. Certainly there is no implied musical connection!

Cross-laterality

The brain works cross-laterally. This means that one side of the brain actually operates the other side of the body. For instance, the right ear communicates with the left side of the brain and similarly the left ear communicates with the right side of the brain. Certain experiments have shown that the use of one ear or the other can affect one's feelings and processing of information. Telephone counsellors are advised to listen with the left ear when they wish to engage the right, intuitive and empathetic brain, the right ear when they wish to receive facts or think logically. Although in most people the analytic hemisphere is on the left side of their brain, most people are right-handed and, since work for most people is connected with analysis, speech and linear thinking, this provides the best connection for them. There is still a scientific view that children are born with equal potential on either side, and that as a child manipulates more with the right hand so the left hemisphere begins to develop a lead, and vice versa. In general hand preference is not finally established until between six and nine years, which would seem to support this view. The brains of right-handed and left-handed people do appear to have slightly different models of organization, but not enough is yet known to be able to apply such knowledge in education.

Even our involuntary eye movements are subject to lateral control, and there has been considerable interest in education in observing these to determine which area of the brain is being drawn upon to answer a question. Researchers claim that if asked to spell a difficult word the majority of people glance up to their right – indicating an engagement of the left brain – whereas when asked to solve a difficult spatial problem the eyes glance up to the left – drawing upon the right brain.

Data suggest that hemispheric specialisation is related to perceptual processing and experience and not merely to the acoustic properties of stimuli.

Hirshkowitz, M. et al. (1978). "EEG alpha asymmetry in musicians and non-musicians: a study of hemispheric specialization", Neuropsychologia, 16.

Laterality effects in audition are not solely determined by stimulus characteristics but are also dependent on task requirements.

Bartholomeus, B. (1974). "Effects of task requirements on ear superiority for sung speech", Cortex, 10, September.

To take just a few examples, we may note the pre-Confucian Chinese concepts of Yin and Yang, the Hindu distinction between "buddhi" and "manas", or C. P. Snow's "two cultures" of the sciences and the arts. Some writers have urged that our materialistic Western culture has forced too great an emphasis on the rational, analytic mode of thought, to the neglect of the intuitive and the holistic. Bruner, for example, suggests that the right hemisphere [of the brain] provides the necessary ingredient for creative thought, an idea enthusiastically pursued and elaborated by Bogen and his colleagues ... Yet hard evidence is lacking ...

Corbalis, M. C. (1976). The Psychology of Left and Right. Hillsdale, NJ: Lawrence Erlbaum Associates.

Right hemisphere functions include "the ability to remember music, nonsense figures, and faces, and to perform a variety of non-verbal, visuo-spatial tasks. … Studies of auditory perception indicate a right hemisphere specialization for the perception of melodies, musical chords, sonar sounds, and environmental sounds; in visual perception, there is a left-hemifield advantage, implying a right hemisphere specialization, for the perception of faces; in tactile perception, the right hemisphere seems to be specialized for the perception of meaningless shapes. The principal characteristic which these right-hemisphere functions share, and which distinguishes them from the corresponding left-hemisphere functions, is that they are non-verbal.

Corbalis, M. C. (1976). The Psychology of Left and Right. Hillsdale, NJ: Lawrence Erlbaum Associates.

The Hopi Indians of the American South West distinguish between the function of their two hands. One hand is for writing and the other is for making music.

Samples (1976).

Recent research into general brain function

Although laterality has been known and written about since Hippocrates in Greece in 400 BC, most of the research and discovery has taken place in the twentieth century. In 1969 J. E. Bogen wrote in the *Los Angeles Neurological Society Bulletin*, "In the human, speaking, reading and writing are largely dependent on one side. While all this is happening on one side of the brain, what is the other side *doing*? I believe it is doing just as much and just as important work. We do not yet understand *how* the one hemisphere produces language; but of the other hemisphere we do not even know *what* it is producing." Brain research has been conducted by neuropsychologists and neurobiologists, and such people have their own thinking processes and their own mental agendas. The work done specifically on music is small in comparison with the whole bulk of brain research. Even the musically biased research depends for its helpfulness very much on the researcher's own analysis of what music is and what makes a musical task. It would be unwise to draw too strong conclusions from it for these reasons alone.

The subjects on which all researchers have experimented in the past have, until the last few decades, been largely those unfortunates in our societies who have suffered brain damage through accident of birth or physical injury. The Russian A. R. Luria, one of the most influential researchers in this field, based his work entirely on patients with lesions or physical damage to or within the brain. He constantly looked at a negative situation from which he could deduce the positive. From what a person whose brain malfunctioned couldn't do, he could deduce what a normal healthy brain could do. From this work we have gained a great deal of what is presently known about essential brain structure.

In a very large proportion of men and women the linguistic/logical hemisphere is situated on the left side of the brain, but in a significant minority of those tested it is on the right. Choosing a useful terminology for left and right brain is therefore difficult. The directional "left" and "right" also raise thoughts of handedness, which is a separate issue, and there is a significant minority of people who function equally well with a reversed structure. I will continue to use the term left brain for the hemisphere that deals with linguistics and logics, and right brain for that which deals with musical sounds, intuition and holistic thought.

Luria identified three principal units of brain function and placed them in hierarchical order. The first he described as the primary area, which is fundamental in that it wakes us up and causes us to be alert. This fundamental function is situated in the "oldest" and deepest part of the brain – the brain stem. The secondary area, which is the outer shell or "cortex", has the function of obtaining, processing and storing information, including visual, auditory and general sensory. The cortex (the word means *bark*, as in tree) is the layer which is divided into the two hemispheres. The third area has an overlapping function, collecting the various signals processed by the varying areas of the cortex and binding them together. It constantly tests, programmes and regulates what it receives, verifying mental activity, and plays a vital role in the conversion of concrete perception into abstract thinking. Both the secondary and tertiary areas are of particular concern to all teachers. Knowledge of the secondary function (hemispheres of the cortex) helps us to begin to utilize some of the unique ways in which different areas of the brain best receive information, and knowledge of the tertiary function (how those hemispheres interact) helps us to understand how important it is to encourage and facilitate interconnectedness of thinking.

Movement

The area of brain process not so far accounted for in Luria's three areas, but of utmost importance to the musician, is that which prepares and controls sensorimotor reaction. In *Taxonomy of Educational Objectives* the educationalist Benjamin Bloom categorizes three equal areas – cognitive, affective and psychomotor. These terms have become widely accepted in the education world and have their uses as shorthand. The first two areas of cognitive and affective correspond to some extent with the left and right hemispheres.

The third term, "psychomotor", has no significant parallel of a separate area or zone of brain function in the cortex. Instead it would appear that both hemispheres link into their own sensorimotor control areas. The particular areas for speech in the left brain, for instance, have elaborate "U"-shaped connections through to the brain stem and to all those systems concerned with the production of speech. Latest research suggests that the cerebellum, located centrally and behind the brain stem and concerned with posture, balance and coordination, may be important in the long-term memorizing of speech and musical movement.

Movement is fundamentally too important to us in our development for it to be confined only to one area of the cortex. Looking at simpler animals with simpler brain structures, we can observe that, although thinking is a very small part of their set up, moving can be extremely sophisticated. The ontology of the brain provides a comparison with that of the evolution of reptiles and the first mammals. We have what some refer to as the reptile brain right down at the base in the central areas of the cerebellum, or substantia nigra. It is deep within here that those essential movement processes are stored. Movement learning is the oldest and most basic learning we experience and it can enhance and modify the effectiveness of both right- and left-brain learning.

There is a great deal of evidence to show that movement learning is fundamentally important to humans, and that we begin to develop sophisticated thought processes in both the right and left brain only through the mediation of movement. This fundamental importance of movement as a specific learning process is best understood by those music educators who work with the very young. Teachers of children of this age can do little musically without working through movement, and in the early years of schooling in any culture, movement learning is fundamental to many areas. As children develop, movement is used by teachers as an important reinforcement of the learning process – finger rhymes would be a good example – and much early music education is inseparable from movement education. It is to our detriment that

The widespread use of the oriental Tai Chi, which stresses a balance in movement and in the flows of energy (*chi*) between both sides of the body and therefore the brain, gives good evidence that some things some of us too easily reject in the West may actually prove to be fundamental to our well-being. The importance of the balance of *chi* is also fundamental to the basis of the practice of acupuncture.

Experiment 1 indicated that newborns who had been exposed to the theme tune of a popular TV programme during pregnancy exhibited changes in heartrate, number of movements and behavioural state 2–4 days after birth. These effects could be attributed to prenatal exposure alone and not to postnatal exposure or a genetic disposition, and were specific to the tune learned.

> Hepper, P. (1991). "An examination of fetal learning before and after birth", Irish Journal of Psychology, 12.

A right ear advantage for speech and a left ear advantage for music were found in the 3 to 5 month olds. However the 2 month olds showed only the music left ear advantage with no reliable evidence of memory-based speech discrimination by either hemisphere. It is suggested that the quality or use of left-hemisphere phonetic memory may change between 2 and 3 months and that the engagement of right-hemisphere specialized memory for musical timbre may precede that for left-hemisphere phonetic memory.

> Best, C, et al. (1982). "Development of infant ear symmetries for speech and music", Perception and Psychophysics, 31, January.

teachers too easily forget the importance of moving as a part of fundamental learning as children grow. All too soon, moving becomes decorative and educationally non-functional and teachers and children ignore it. Work in music therapy clearly shows the vital part that education of and through psychomotor control plays with adults as well as children. It acts as a constant reminder to us that therapy is not merely medicinally helpful to those in distress or special need, but is fundamental to all of us.

In the first weeks of life, alongside the appreciation of melody and its concomitant rhythmic structures, psychomotor control patterns are the earliest to be established and are founded deep within our brains.

The two hemispheres deal with psychomotor learning in very different ways. Music educators will be very aware of these contrasting types of sensorimotor learning in instrumental teaching. Action which has been accessed through the right brain has a different effect from that which has been accessed through the left.

The best performers commit a great deal of what they do to their long-term memories, learning not through a process of logical analysis but through a combination of repetitive movement and right-brain properties of contour and aural perception. Student candidates in formal harmony examinations could often be observed "playing" on an imaginary keyboard on the exam room desk in order to solve the best part-writing in the set task, because they had learnt the procedures as movements and overall shapes. Only when they made these movements were they then able to subject them to cognitive analysis. Since the right brain does not respond to analysis, indeed does not recognize it, it stores shapes and procedures in their entirety. Such students had learnt to create an aural perception of appropriate sounds internally through movement.

Although the processes of committing things to the long-term memory are not yet at all well understood, we do know that the hard repetitive work it involves is worth it. The long-term memory stores information which can be retrieved and examined, deconstructed and analysed at will. Western educational practices tend to rely far more on the storage of memories in the written word or graphic symbol, ignoring the long-term memory, and this can mean that without these cues we are powerless to act. Far too many musicians in our society fall into this category and are unable to fulfil musical tasks when they are divorced from notation, either re-creating the music of others or improvising.

Research into how brain function can affect musical behaviour

An important field of research into brain and music, found mostly in universities in the United States and Canada over the last forty years, has specialized in setting up simple tasks with groups of people – often volunteer students – and observing how these tasks are completed by differentiated groups. Sometimes these groups will be people whose linguistic/logical brain function is known to be on the left side; in other cases students with certain types of educational experiences will be tested against others with a contrasting set of experiences. For music educators some of the most interesting are those experiments which contrast the ways in which both music students and science students approach certain problem-solving tasks. At the moment evidence shows that, in laboratory circumstances, music students are better able to coordinate both hemispheres of their brain than are science students. There is also evidence to show that musicians tend to use their left brains more actively in performing musical tasks in comparison with non-musicians.

Music educators should not take this as too much of a compliment, since it also highlights a weakness in our teaching. The likely cause is that Western music education at the higher levels at present particularly accentuates left-brain learning, and at its best provides a good balance between the actual sounds (right brain) and the logics that connect them (left brain), whereas science education relies mostly on written and factual information and does not encourage much intuitive thought except at the higher levels. This is a worry, perhaps, also for science educators. Unfortunately, too often the left-brain work in music is not well enough counterbalanced and students too easily lose their connection with essential and basic right-brain skills related to the manipulation and perception of sound.

A new and revolutionary type of brain research has only recently come on stream. The invention of Positron Emission Tomography has at last allowed researchers to study brain action at the moment it takes place. Research using these techniques has been available only in recent years but it has enormously increased knowledge of how the brain works. The individual under inspection receives an injection of a slightly radioactive form of glucose. The glucose is absorbed by brain cells so that the most is assimilated by the most active cells. This absorption can be detected by the specialized scanner. The resultant colour slides demonstrate actual hemispheral activity most startlingly. Some famous early examples of such scans show the brain receiving both language and music. What is clear is that during speech reception the left side of the brain is highly active and the right side minimally active. When the brain is stimulated by music the right side is highly active, and the left side remains active but at a somewhat lower level.

More recently the combination of computers and brain research has led to the use of topographical brain mapping of the brain's electrical activity. This work does not involve any form of intrusion and is likely to provide some of the most revealing insights into how we process music. Dr Steve Brown of Manchester Royal Infirmary has already shown how the brains of those listening to music involve the right and left hemispheres differently according to the type of stimulus. Paul Robertson's (1993) account of Dr Brown's work suggests some fascinating new things which have much to recommend to us as teachers.

Brown's experiments, still in process, show that the left and right hemispheres react separately to musical stimulus. The right becomes excited by concordant sounds whereas the left is stimulated by discords. Our appreciation of octaves, fourths and fifths is therefore linked with the understanding of overall rhythmic procedures and tonal centres and allies itself with our intuitive, spiritual thinking processes, while that of sevenths and seconds is allied with logic and formal, arhythmic, objective and rational thinking. This new

In a test for brain preference indicators the following questions are asked.
Do you learn athletics and dancing better by:

a) imitating, getting the feel of the music or game?
b) learning the sequence and repeating the steps mentally?

By their nature, some sports invite more comparisons and evaluations than others and are preferred by the left dominants. Lefts like to "play" competitively, whether it's in the garden or on the golf course. Their flowers are entered in shows and their scores posted on the club notice board. Rights thrive on freedom and dread comparison; when they play tennis they simply enjoy hitting the ball, and their hikes have no destination in mind. When lefts play tennis they prefer to start scoring faster. And a hike less than ten miles is to them a failure. These same tendencies towards competitiveness and goal-setting versus recreation for relaxation and having fun are also evident in work. The thrill of doing is enough for the right-brained person, but the left wants a product to result from crafts and gardening.

Wonder, J. and Donovan, P. (1984). Whole Brain Thinking. New York: William Morrow.

Right hemispheral specialization has been demonstrated for musical functions. Experts, however, showed greater disruption with the right hand. This supports the hypothesis of a leftward shift of hemispheric specialization for the performance of musical tasks after academic musical training.

Fabbro, F. et al. (1990). "Opposite musical-manual interference in young vs expert musicians", Neuropsychologia, 28.

Music students and science students use similar cerebral hemispheric dominant and right preferences for problem solving but musicians are more likely to use an integrated processing mode than science students. Science students are more likely to use left processing mode.

Chesson, D. et al. (1993). "Hemispheric preferences for problem solving in a group of music majors and computer science majors," Instructional Psychology, 20, June.

The neural correlates of music perception were studied by measuring cerebral blood flow changes with positron emission tomography … We conclude that specialized neural systems in the right superior temporal cortex participate in perceptual analysis of melodies; pitch comparisons are effected via a neural network that includes right prefrontal cortex, but active retention of pitch involves the interaction of right temporal and frontal cortices.

Evans, A. et al. (1994). "Neural mechanisms underlying melodic perception and memory for pitch", Journal of Neuroscience, 14, April.

information produces a parallel with the growth and development of music in society that cannot easily be ignored. From the beginning of Western musical history the unison, fourth, fifth and octave have been identified as spiritual in effect, and the development of discord over the last seven hundred years in Western Europe suggests an increasingly left-brain function in the creation of music. This same span of time also contains the evolution of notation, and the two appear to go hand in hand. This opposition of the intuitive musical response of right brain and the linear cognition of the left brain provides the clearest evidence yet of a reason why many musicians still experience some opposition between sound and symbol, between the use of aural memory and notation. If we are to maximize our whole brain then we need to learn to be able to function in both ways and to synthesize the results. There is clear evidence that complex music is perceived and enjoyed through whole-brain action, whereas simple music engages only the right brain.

Robertson (1993) also explains how his work with Dr Peter Fenwick, consultant neuropsychiatrist at Maudsley and Bethlehem Hospital, London, suggests that different styles of music will demand a more right- or left-brain approach both from the composer and the listener. Whereas the present interest in the music of Gorecki, Pärt or Tavener accentuates right-brain function through use of tonality, concord and intuitive processes, causing strong emotional reactions in listeners, the music of Boulez, Birtwistle or Maxwell Davies conversely is founded on dissonance and accentuates left-brain processes, stimulating arhythmic and atonal properties and engaging the listener at an objective and intellectual level. The emotional states aroused by right-brain music can be explained in part by the stimulus it provides to the right brain's limbic system. The limbic system is an "old" part of the brain's structure which borders on the corpus callosum and is concerned with basic emotion, spiritual experience, hunger and sex.

There is now evidence to show that the music we hear between the ages of eight and eleven has the strongest influence on us and is stored by the brain in complete detail. It is based on the fact that several patients with a lesion in one small area of the brain suffer an involuntary total recall of all the music heard between these ages. The significance of this research finding to teachers at Key Stage 2 is enormous, showing the vital part played by music education in upper primary work. The need to involve children in a broad range of quality musical experiences is at its most pressing at this time, when what children listen to outside the school must be enhanced and balanced by what they can experience inside.

Music education's uniqueness as schooling for the brain

The early notions of left- and right-brain teaching, which appeared first in California in the late 1960s and early 1970s, were a useful guide to teachers and demonstrated the need to encourage the use of the whole of the brain in teaching. In those very early days there were always warnings. A typical response came from Dr Frank R. Wilson, an assistant clinical professor of neurology at the University of California School of Medicine. In a paper written in 1985 he warned that, although observations and theories about lateralized specialization of the brain have improved our understanding of the complexity of our own mental functioning, he felt too unsure at that point about the actual processes to permit such concepts to become a basis for the guiding principles in education.

Instead he emphasized the intimate connection between ear and bodily function and the unique part music education has to play in cementing this relationship.

Everything we have learnt in the last ten years has reinforced this interrelationship of brain function and the subsequent interaction with bodily action. Alongside this we are becoming increasingly aware of the ability the brain has to process different things in different ways and how we, as educators, may learn to help these processes to interact more fully.

A strong case can be made for the inclusion of music in any general curriculum because of some special features of the human brain and the muscular system to which it is bonded. Like all moving creatures, we have a central nervous system that regulates the body in its interactions with the outside world. Because we are primates – that is, mammals who walk upright – our upper limbs are not used to support our body weight against gravity. With this mechanical change in posture in relation to gravity, there has existed for mankind the opportunity to use the hands and arms for an endless variety of specialized tasks. Co-existing with that opportunity, we find an enormous elaboration in the brain of a motor control system that seems dedicated to permitting extraordinary refinement of movement of our upper limbs. We also have the gift of exceptional control of the muscles of the face and oral cavity, and the brain mechanisms for controlling the muscles just as precisely as we control those of the upper limbs. What makes us special in the biological sense, in other words, is the unique control we have of our upper limbs and vocal apparatus, and the linkage of these capabilities to a strong urge to communicate to ourselves and to others around us.

Making music involves the full exercise of these innate and special human capabilities. And this, I think, is the crux of the education issue. If you seek to encourage young people to develop themselves in a way that fortifies their natural curiosity and leads to a refinement in physical and mental ability, why not provide opportunities suited to the gifts granted by our biological heritage? Music is not only the effective primer for the developing mind and body, but it is an exacting and progressive blend of scientific, artistic, and physical disciplines that can be undertaken and enjoyed at an early age, and it is one whose long-range value will not depend on the ultimate pursuit of a musical career.

Wilson (1985).

If there are secrets to be learnt about good music teaching they are in the identification and enhancement of this area of interaction of brain functions. The complex interrelationships between the left brain, the right brain and the psychomotor must concern music educators as much as, if not more than, most other educators. Unique among the traditional subject areas, music utilizes all these in good if not equal measure. Western educational systems concentrate largely on verbal and intellectual training. The current debate about the importance of the "three r's" – which are largely left-brain oriented – is nothing new, nor is this uniquely a British concern. Arts teachers and music educators in particular have an important task in maintaining the balance in developing brain activity in children.

Despite the fact that music displays itself "in time", the temporal perceptual task of the listener who hears the recurring rhythmic clusters of a popular tune is quite simple: it consists in merely discovering and identifying a musical segment of very short duration that consists of repetition of a rhythmic, melodic or timbral pattern with hardly any harmonic, instrumental, or contrapuntal complexity. Hardly any analysis of the information is needed, and usually the perceptual task is performed well by the right hemisphere …

… Executive functions (i.e. singing, complex rhythmic tasks) are fundamentally dependent on serial temporal and *sequential* organization and may depend on processing systems that were lateralized very early.

Martin (1982).

Not everyone agrees of course …

What we should be striving for is not the pampering of one hemisphere to the neglect of the other (whether left or right) or their independent development, but the marriage and harmony of the two. It so happens that special territories of the right – spatial perception, pictorial recognition and intuitive thought – are not easily amenable to conventional education, nor is it clear that they would benefit from years of formal instruction. Systems of education, especially higher education (and this applies to every culture), seem designed to develop and exploit the powers of the hemisphere that is dominant for speech, for those powers depend most on factual knowledge and prolonged training … To ignore the dominant and to encourage the minor side to take charge may produce deleterious consequences in behaviour. It could cause problems as profound as the disorders of emotion and speech.

Blakemore, C. (1977). Mechanics of the Mind. Cambridge: Cambridge University Press.

Musical training improves processing of tonality in the left hemisphere.

Perstedt, P. et al. (1989). "Musical training improves processing of tonality in the left hemisphere", Music Perception, 6, Spring.

This finding suggests that musical timbre perception, examined in a psychoacoustic sense, depends on neural systems found within the right temporal lobe.

Samson, S. and Zatorre, R. J. (1994). "Contribution of the right temporal lobe to musical timbre discrimination", Neuropsychologia, 32, 2.

These results support the idea that imagery arises from activation of a neural substrate shared with perceptual mechanisms, and provides evidence for a right temporal-lobe specialization for this type of auditory processing.

Halpern, A and Zatorre, R. J. (1993). "Effect of unilateral temporal-lobe excision on perception and imagery of songs", Neuropsychologia, 31, 3.

The power of music over us from infancy to the grave is so great that those of us who try to establish a closer intimacy between this powerful force and the plastic child have assumed a serious, even if the most joyful, undertaking. For "Thus", says Stanley Hall, "in a day when the psychologists are realizing with one accord that the feelings are far vaster than the intellect and will, and are more important for health and sanity, it is clear that music teachers more than any other class are charged with the custody and responsibility of the hygiene of the emotional life."

Coleman (1922).

The really valuable thing is intuition.

Albert Einstein

As yet we do not possess any large-scale training systems for the development of right-brain thinking, and as more information comes to light it will be necessary to adapt and change those things we already do. But it would be foolish to disregard what research is showing us now and not to try to make some use of the facts that emerge merely because we are as yet uncertain about the whole picture. In describing music education in action in our schools and colleges I will seek also to show how this knowledge of bi-lateral function can enhance the effectiveness of teaching. Musical stimulus normally starts from the right brain. Teachers must plan their work to make certain that the right-brain functions are given preferential treatment so that the sound (right brain) may precede the symbol (left brain).

Resumé

- Both teachers and children need to be aware of which parts of their brains can do which kinds of tasks.

- We are accustomed to thinking and feeling but concentrate only on educating thinking, whereas feeling may actually dominate decisions. Arts education must be concerned with both.

- The three active modes are thinking, feeling and doing. We can learn to use those parts of our brain we wish to focus upon. Our brains are flexible and we are in control of them. Learning to stimulate and engage brain processes appropriately lies at the heart of good teaching.

- The brain has two hemispheres connected by the corpus callosum. The left hemisphere is dominant in our society since it promotes verbal reasoning, computation and logic. It is objective and analytical. The right hemisphere promotes intuition and feeling response and reacts to visual and aural stimulus, processing overall shapes and contours. It is subjective and holistic and understands metaphor.

- The brain works cross-laterally. Handedness is a separate issue and has its own mechanisms.

- Luria proposed three brain areas: the primary is the waking brain, the secondary the cortical processes, and the third and most important the tertiary area, which binds the work of all areas of the brain together.

- The cognitive and affective can be seen somewhat as function of left and right hemispheres respectively, but the psychomotor is not a separate area. Rather each hemisphere has its own motor systems. Movement is of fundamental importance to us in the learning process.

- Along with identification of melodic contour, movement is the earliest kind of learning and goes on in the womb. Music education appears to enhance cross-lateral thinking more so than science education.

- Positron Emission Tomography and topographical brain mapping have recently greatly enlarged our understanding of how the brain processes music. It can be shown that the right brain responds to concord, the left brain to discord, and this fundamentally affects the way we approach differing kinds of music. It can also be shown that the right brain's limbic system is activated by certain kinds of music.

- Children between eight and eleven are likely to retain total recall of all the music they experience and to be able to recall it in detail in later life.

- In teaching, the principle of sound first, working from the overall to the particular, should help gain a balance between right- and left-brain thinking. In using movement to enhance musical learning, repetition is an important factor.

- Music is a unique schooling for the brain, involving both right- and left-brain processes wedded together through fine and disciplined movement.

Contour (recognized by right brain) is an important grouping factor in pitch sequences and laterality effects are useful.

Peretz, I. (1992). "The role of contour and intervals in the recognition of melody parts: evidence from cerebral asymmetries in musicians", Neuropsychologia, 30, March.

Teaching implications

Music teachers must consider carefully how they can stimulate right-brain procedures, since they will more naturally use left-brain procedures in initiating projects. If we teach through metaphor we engage the right brain, since the left brain does not understand metaphor. We can make certain that sound itself, shape, colour, contour, spatial concepts and other right-brain procedures are stimulated by the lesson content. First is an example of a lesson which starts from a visual metaphor but which also requires analytical thinking. Lessons of this type can be found in John Paynter's *Sound and Structure* (1991).

Example 1

An "A"-Level specialist music class is presented with a reproduction of Piet Mondriaan's painting *Broadway Boogie-Woogie* without being told the title. They are asked to improvise a piece of music lasting two minutes based on this picture using only their voices (with or without words) and body percussion. Having done this and evaluated the experience they are then asked to repeat the piece using only percussion instruments. After a further evaluation they are asked to repeat the piece a third time using their own first instruments. The final challenge is to produce a composite score by writing down their own individual parts and then amalgamating them using an overhead projector.

Example 2

A secondary class of Year 8 pupils (12 years old) is asked to consider the overall structure of a musical extract by listening to it only. They must engage the right brain to enable them to detect large structural groupings and sub-groupings. Further and more detailed questioning about the naming of constituent parts and a precise analysis of the relative lengths and contents will engage an increasing interaction between left and right brain. The teacher records decisions on the blackboard or overhead projector and builds up the opening of a graphic score for the piece. The introduction of some musical notation, if the class is familiar with it as a system, to identify major themes will further strengthen the left's role, since this is the area which understands and processes the logics of reading. A synthesis of right- and left-brain learning should result. Each child is asked to "map" this music across a page from left to right, inserting the appropriate notation at the apposite place. The piece is played several times as they do this.

Example 3

A contrasting example from a lesson with young children will be familiar to most music educators. They will know that it is possible to teach a song to young children by imitation, or rote, and for the pupils to learn both the melody and the words without having any idea what the words mean. Many young children can sing "Frère Jacques" without the slightest knowledge of French. The words have been stored as sounds in the sound-processing right brain and are open to the analysis of the speech areas of the left brain only when and if they become meaningful.

Example 4

A university teacher sets a group the task of listening to a piece they have never heard before. At the first listening they are asked to do nothing but think of a central image or name or symbol for this unidentified piece of music. They are encouraged not to decide on this until the end of the piece and then to draw or write their image in the centre of a large sheet of paper. They are then asked to listen to the piece again at least twice and to begin to make a web diagram of the music with their image at the centre. They proceed by noting down anything they hear in any way whatsoever. They are encouraged to use music notation when easy and appropriate, to use statements of analogy, descriptive simile and metaphor, and also technical musicological language. A discussion follows about the structure, expressive content and overall effectiveness of the chosen piece. In this way both the left and right brain are stimulated equally and the student will be encouraged to interact swiftly between one hemisphere and the other. A further emphasis on the left brain can be encouraged by isolating a short section of the piece and employing this for aural dictation using pencil graphics on score paper. Repeated listenings allow students gradually to fill in the score using conventional notation wherever they can. The two combined papers will provide a very useful insight into each student's capabilities in overall musical brain terms.

Example 5

In a rehearsal of a sextet of mine, the professional performing group arrived at bars of 11/8 for which the conductor could not find the right conducting gesture. The rehearsal broke down several times until the trumpeter, Elgar Howarth, suggested a way out. Just say "Gary Howarth used to play the xylophone", he proposed. This was adopted, and the rehearsal continued having conquered that problem. During the performance, a page before the offending bars, the conductor made a grandiose sweep of the hand and the page containing the 11/8 figures floated to the floor. His conducting gesture stopped momentarily and the 11/8 bars flowed through without a hitch.

Commentary

In Example 1 the right brain is dominantly engaged in the opening processes, and as the lesson proceeds the left brain becomes increasingly important in producing a synthesis or synergy. Example 2 works from the overall sound and shape of the music, perceived largely by the right brain, to smaller structural detail engaging left-brain focus. Example 3 is almost entirely right-brain oriented, and in Example 4 the students are encouraged to use both sides of the brain. Music education practice in higher education can be so strongly word- and notation-biased that this kind of lesson will encourage students with good musical ability but poorer verbal skills to maximize what they have.

If we teach from the sound of music first, the right brain is most likely to be engaged initially, since it is the principal receptor of musical sounds. In the case of strongly atonal or dissonant music the reverse applies. As the questions themselves make it necessary to move from overall understanding to an analysis of parts, so left-brain processes will strengthen. If the lesson has started with atonal or dissonant music it will be important to work from the intellectual response of the left brain and gradually to engage the intuitive response through repeated listenings, allowing the right brain gradually to absorb the shapes and contours and memorize them. As this process of familiarization takes place the student's emotional reaction is much more likely to become more positive, whereas first reactions are more likely to be negative.

At every level of music education it is important to use a variety of strategies to engage left, right and psychomotor learning. Musical activities must first be accessed through sound and first thoughts should always be formed by the actual sound itself. But students need to be encouraged to think and to explore and to examine detail, aided when appropriate by notation. Because listening with notation engages more left-brain activity, the actual effect of the music on the student changes in comparison with listening without access to notation.

The use of mnemonics, engaging left-brain techniques to provide logics enabling the right brain to grasp an overall pattern, is a common teaching device. It works well in these circumstances but is so powerful in its effect that it is tempting for teachers to use mnemonics for all rhythmic phrases and to produce a kind of substitute language that puts the left brain too well in control. In nineteenth-century France, a mnemonic system was formalized from that used by the French army to teach their drummers basic rhythms. The resulting "French Time Names" (taa, ta-té, ta-fa-te-fi, etc.) have been used much in music education in the past to help right-brain patterns establish through systemized left-brain procedures.

Learning through moving: repetition as a necessary technique

Musical learning is considerably enhanced and reinforced by the application of movement. Moving to music is natural and an important part of our early and later learning process. Perception of pulse and metre can be enhanced by dancing, but so also can perception of melodic contour, texture, phrase and cadence. In fact there is nothing that you can hear in music that cannot somehow be expressed in movement. Dance occurs in all cultures and is closely linked to the expressive function of music and to our right brain's perception of large musical structures. Repetition is a vital part of musical learning and is a central technique for linking movement with music.

Simple repetition, allowing the brain to absorb what it needs in time, is not a favoured method of access of information in our society. Today speed is of the essence, and we always seek for short cuts. In learning about music the less we repeat the actual music in time, the more we rely on reading information *about* it. This can be in the form of written words or music notation. In both cases the reception and absorption of such information is through the left brain, whereas the absorption of music in performance in time is accessed through the right brain.

Every time you have a thought, the biochemical/electromagnetic resistance along the pathway carrying that thought is reduced. It is like trying to clear a path through the forest. The first time is a struggle because you have to fight your way through the undergrowth. The second time you travel that way will be easier because of the clearing you did on your first journey. The more times you travel that path, the less resistance there will be, until, after many repetitions, you have a wide, smooth track which requires little or no clearing. A similar function occurs in your brain: the more you repeat patterns of maps of thought, the less resistance there is to them. Therefore, and of greater significance, *repetition in itself increases the probability of repetition*. In other words, the more times a "mental event" happens, the more likely it is to happen.

Buzan (1989).

Right hemisphere has superior ability to generate and/or manipulate echoic images in the memory.

O'Boyle, M. et al. (1990). "How knowledge of the song influences the matching of melodies to rhythm sequences tapped in the left and right palms", Cortex, 26, December.

Results suggest that associative auditory functions that generate expectancies for harmonic progression in music are lateralized within the right hemisphere.

Tramo, M. et al. (1991). "Musical priming by the right hemisphere post-callosotomy", Neuropsychologia, 29.

From research into the education of the memory we can begin to learn how best to approach the development of the musical memory in young children. Alongside musical listening, general listening skills are being developed, and both are subject to similar processes. Simple repetition is fundamental to both. The following lesson uses both movement and repetition to engage right-brain melodic, harmonic and rhythmic perceptions. Left-brain procedures are built up as these devices are named. Movement assists and strengthens both types of learning.

Example 6

In a secondary school a Year 9 class is played a recording of a calypso from Trinidad, *Panamam Tombé,* and is asked to learn this song by rote. The teacher uses hand gestures, including sol-fa signs, to reinforce the melodic shape of each line as the song is repeated several times. The class is then asked to identify the fundamental steady beat by walking round the room in a circle precisely in time with this beat. As they become able to do this the teacher asks them to sing the song as well. The teacher then asks them to stand still in the circle and to tap on their knees the half beats. The song is repeated and the pupils now walk, sing and tap. The class's attention is drawn to the calypso rhythm pattern played on the claves. This 1, 4, 7 pattern occurs on half beats. When it has been identified and analysed by the pupils as beats 1, 4 and 7, they are asked to step the steady beat, click their fingers on the calypso pattern and sing the song as well. Lastly the class is asked to stand in a circle, listen to the song and identify the two chords in the accompaniment. The first chord is identified as Chord 1 by the teacher and the other as Chord Something-Else. The pupils are asked to raise their left hand when they hear Chord 1 and their right hand when they hear Chord Something-Else. Having done this the class is asked to use this information in walking to the steady beat. They are told that when they hear Chord 1 they must walk clockwise and when they hear Chord Something-Else they must turn smartly and proceed anti-clockwise. Clicking the calypso pattern and singing the song as well would perfect the performance with a talented and willing class! It can be seen how this lesson attempts to synergize all musical brain areas in thinking, listening, feeling and doing.

In our time-bound society, where watching the clock dominates, it is fascinating to observe the continuing success of composers whose music accentuates timelessness and uses repetition as a principle. The music of Glass, Adams and Nyman all relies on repetition and its power to communicate with those parts of our brains that are undernourished by the left-brain dominated demands of today.

ADVANTAGING THE EAR

3

What is the "ear"?

Our ears are the collectors of music and our brain receives, understands, perceives and codifies music. The ear, when receiving sounds and not words, is the channel leading to the right brain, which understands sounds as music. When musicians talk about "the ear" they refer mostly to that part of our thinking and feeling system which deals with music. Very rarely are they concerned with the ear itself in the way in which, say, a physical educationist might be concerned with the leg. The term often used to describe musical brain function is "the inner ear", but this is also biologically confusing. Music educators use the term "internalize" to describe hearing in the mind.

The central issue outlined in the first chapter was the sounding symbol and the nature of real musical experience. Sound and its symbol; the intangible and the here and now; thinking and feeling; logic and metaphor; technique and perception; all these pairs acknowledge that duality within our brains which teachers must strive to understand. With this understanding they must attempt to facilitate a synthesis of opposites through action, making sounding symbols. Making certain that the sound comes before its symbol means giving a clear preference to aural perception and memory, and this is how we give the ear an advantage and help the process of internalization. Most aural work with children will come in through the right brain, and we need to recognize and be wary of our left-brained adult obsession with words, symbols and writing when introducing children to music. Teachers must try to use written symbols to enhance the right brain's perceptions, not to replace them.

From the very first lessons in school or in the instrumental studio, teachers must find ways of giving the ear, the memory and the right brain the lion's share of emphasis and stimulus. This way musical experience becomes the true focus of the teaching. For example, classes of very young children being taught songs need to have their attention focused on the melodic and rhythmic shapes of their songs, with less emphasis on the meaning of the words. Hand actions which emphasize the rhythmic patterns and melodic contours can be taught as well as those that underline or emphasize the meaning of the words, which are more common. Teachers will need to think of ways in which they can still deliver their cross-curricular reinforcement, for instance of number, and still strengthen the musical patterns. A number song that uses fingers for the numbers can also use a stepped gesture in the air to indicate pitch contour.

A child beginning to play an instrument, let's say a recorder, needs first to concentrate only on the action which produces the melodic phrase, which is learnt from the teacher's example and the aural memory of that sound. Shutting their eyes and listening first and feeling how the

An infants' teacher may teach the song "The Little Boy of the Sheep" using hand actions to emphasize the word meaning, for example, looking gestures, guarding gestures, piping gestures, or may alternatively teach the gently descending contour gestures emphasizing the melodic contour and finishing on a strong tonic gesture for at least some of the salient parts of the melody.

action goes will help pupils to concentrate this as a right-brain process. Bringing left-brain action such as notation reading into the learning situation at the same time provides unnecessarily worrying cross-brain reaction before the sound and its appropriate action is secure. Accentuating the musical memory advantages the ear and therefore the right brain most strongly. As the pupil becomes secure and at one with the instrument, able to express themselves on it by manipulating sounds, able to make their own patterns as well as remembering many taught patterns, then the notation symbols can be introduced as needed. Children's memories are so extraordinarily efficient at primary age that it is verging on the criminal to set them immediately upon a path that leads them away from musical memory and binds them to the crutch of notation for ever. Teaching beginner instrumentalists in this way should allow the teacher to focus the pupils on the actual sound they produce, and feel the movements they are making, helping them to hear when they are in tune and when not, as well as achieving phrasing and all those other articulations that make playing musical.

Musical listening

The English language provides different words for hearing and listening, and the second, "listening", is the term used prevalently in music education since it implies focused or concentrated attention. But musical listening is a certain and distinct kind of listening very different from, for instance, speech listening. It has its own dedicated set of brain functions. By putting the ear first we provide the greatest opportunity for students to engage that part of the brain which responds to sound *per se* and thus to store overall musical shapes. We can also listen with our cognitive left-brain facilities, but then we listen for different things – only those things that we can name, analyse and symbolize. Listening for and to the properties of sound itself and memorizing them provides the best aural record of the experience and the basis for comparison with future repeated hearings. The first time we hear a new piece we are bound to listen to it mainly as sound. We take in the overall shapes, strong feelings of communication, and brief memories of rhythm, melodic contour, tone colour, texture, harmony and so on. Because the music moves rapidly in time, our logical processes hardly have time to analyse and operate upon the information. That requires repeated listenings building upon the sound memories from before.

We all know what it feels like to meet a piece of music for the first time and how vague and fleeting the experience can often be. Before we try to analyse and break down this strange information into logical sequences with formal names it is best to do something active in order to internalize the experience. The need for actual physical action is most keenly felt by the young. They need to know what it feels like. Such action may be merely showing the steady beat or the pattern of the metre; it might be performing motifs or figures akin to those to be listened to, or it could be moving expressively. As we grow older and we have memories of what physically becoming involved in music can be like, we can rely on that memory somewhat, instead of the actuality. We know what it feels like and can access that memory without necessarily going through the process, but, even so, active involvement always produces a deeper understanding. Even as adults we learn best by doing.

Gaining musical experience

Before undergoing any formal learning a pupil must gain a wide experience of music as a listener and as an active participant (remember particularly the importance of the ages of eight to eleven). This widening experience must continue throughout the whole of music education. When we listen to music with an active brain, that is, engaging both sides in synthesis, we are using part of our body actively, and such active listening is also implied in this principle. Anyone who has taken part in musical activities knows that listening without the underlying experience of truly active participation is differently fulfilling. To know music well you have to "do it", and such doing provides the best foundation for internalization and holistic musical perception.

A hallmark of the developments in British music education over the last thirty years has been in active participation of pupils in the musical experience. There have been some very localized British developments of Orff's ideas, particularly applied to the use of pitched percussion, but rarely is it taken beyond the initial stage. Kodály's vocal method has had a rather more significant effect, perhaps reawakening memories in some teachers of Sol-fa teaching during the first half of the twentieth century. Sol-fa was first properly codified for general use by music educators in Britain in the 1840s, but despite this the system tends to be seen as, at best, a helpful parallel system. Both Orff and Kodály's methods have aural experience as a central issue, although Kodály introduces notation much earlier than Orff. Above all a "pupil-centred" methodology has evolved which encourages fundamental musical experience as creator, receiver and re-creator. Without hours of musical experience, and an active storing of this through various forms of physically enhanced learning, there is little or no hope of developing the enormous musical potential of the brain and properly advantaging the ear.

What makes an effective musician?

So much of our Western style of music teaching is done through the visual symbolizing of music, whether in words or in various forms of notation. The dominance of the book as a way of learning in the Western world has helped to lead to a similar overbalance in the learning of essential music skills such as singing and instrumental performance. In contrast the most effective and multi-skilled practical musicians in our society are mostly those who have approached music through these first three principles. They have learnt to play

- by absorbing enormous quantities of musical stimulus
- by letting what they hear guide them to what they want to do
- by approaching the reproduction of this music through using sensori-motor skills guided by aural acuity.

If we were able to have a complete census of all people of school age who this year play an instrument or sing, we would find that this type

Pupils should be helped to develop their understanding and enjoyment of music through a balanced programme of activities which provides opportunities for them to work individually, in groups and as a class.

SCAA (1994). Music in the National Curriculum: Draft Proposals.

From his work in the Günther School in Munich in 1924, the composer Carl Orff (1895–1982) developed an interest in music education which became formalized into a method called "Orff Schulwerk". Aurally based, the method used simplified pitch-percussion instruments combined with singing and wind and stringed instruments to facilitate easy participation in music by non-skilled performers. As in his composing style, he revelled in repeated figures, drones and simple melodic devices using modal scales, formalizing these into a progressive series of exercises as exemplars for teachers. Although the exercises are notated for teachers, they are taught by rote.

The Hungarian composer Zoltan Kodály (1882-1987) formalized a method of music teaching founded on his studies of folk music. From 1908 to 1914 he was closely involved in forming the music curriculum in Hungarian schools. His method is vocally based and provides notated sight-reading materials written and arranged from folk sources by the composer. Children learn to sight-sing in parts from a very young age. Kodály utilized the elements of Sol-fa as a basis for his work with children.

of musician would be by far the most prevalent, ranging from the child recorder player to the folk guitarist and the sophisticated rock drummer. Teachers must respect and acknowledge aurally based skills acquired by many pupils, challenging them to improve and refine these skills rather than to change to a notation-based system, helping them to learn to record only what they need when they need it. Such pupils should also be strongly involved in scan-reading notation in listening sessions, and this will assure them a foundation upon which to build notational skills if they wish at any later stage to develop them further.

Despite their many years of intensive work, many students reaching postgraduate status in music can feel that they have been severely disadvantaged by their formal music education. Even given the advantages of cross-brain ability acquired through their subject teaching, after sometimes twenty years of specialist music teaching many find themselves unable to perform without notation, which is often so significantly called "my music". Their repertoire is often small and of little application to the world of music at large. At the end of three or four years' intensive higher study their musical memory can remain largely undeveloped. Their ability to listen to a piece of music and to reproduce it either on their instrument or as musical notation is rarely developed at all, despite intensive practice during public examination courses and in tertiary and higher education through elements called "musicianship" or "aural training". The general ineffectiveness of such courses and the subsequent stigmatizing and loss of self-respect of music graduates is one of the most serious deficiencies of our present system of music education. It can be clearly traced back to the ear, therefore the right brain, not being allowed to be the central focus of their music education, to the lack of development of their musical memory and critical aural perception and to the overdependence on left-brain procedures linked to notation and the written word.

Stimulating the ear

A rule of thumb to allow us to provide the right brain with advantage and also to stimulate the left brain emerges as

- first engage the ear through action (right brain)
- next move to analysis through action (right to left)
- finally achieve synthesis through action (both).

Music must be heard to be understood, but in the upper reaches of education, from secondary school onwards, it is not uncommon to find many sessions taught without music being heard. This is not uncommon in examination work, when there is pressure of time because of very full examination syllabuses. To study music without hearing it and listening to it can lead to lack of sensitivity to music, to false judgements about it and to faulty perceptions of it. Above all it can produce students at the end of the education system who are frustrated by their own lack of fundamental musical skills and who find difficulty in synthesizing their personal experience of music with what they have been taught.

As musical memory and musical experience develop it becomes gradually more possible to engage in some musical discourse without the physical presence of sound, since the appropriate sounds can be already stored in the long-term memory in such a way as to be accessible and analysable at will. As this becomes possible, music education discourse can centre more on notation and written commentaries, but the actual physical presence of music heard in time must never be far away.

The present British system of higher education, however, tends badly to overestimate the ability of most music students to achieve this soundless functioning state, yet very little attempt is made by higher education teachers to facilitate and develop this ability. The system often expects students to produce aesthetic response without the impetus of physical sound, and in doing so demands of the majority of students a skill that is too rarely found. Far too many students graduating from BA, BMus and BEd courses cannot rely solely on their ear for fundamental musical decisions, cannot easily identify intervals or detect faults in rehearsal, cannot analyse complex harmony aurally, and are lost as performers without easy and constant access to notation because they have not formed strong enough cross-brain connections between the sound and its symbol.

At a recent national music education conference, a university professor of music gave a lecture which started with the writing up on a board of copious musical examples in notation. It became clear that a large part of his audience, although all with high music qualifications, could not create the sound of the examples accurately enough in their heads to follow his thesis, whereas he, knowing the music in question in detail, was perfectly able to. The main thrust of his argument was therefore lost on the audience and the lecture began to antagonize them.

Thinking about music

Although music educators working with very young children are not likely to make the mistake of ignoring real musical stimulus, on the other hand they can be less aware of the need to engage the children's thinking process as they listen, moving to the second principle of analysis through action. Some teachers rarely help their pupils to penetrate beyond the outer layer of factual information about music – most commonly the instrumentation. This can instil in pupils a "spotter's guide" mentality ("there goes the oboe"), whereby a musical performance becomes largely a checking-off of instrumental colours noticed. Far more importantly, the teacher needs to engage the pupils' attention on the inner workings of music – those elements from which it is constructed – and how these relate to style and function. A balance between listening to music and thinking about it helps to achieve that heightened awareness which synthesis between thinking and feeling can create.

Musicians can function away from the stimulus of actual sound. If we examine critically the perceptual skills needed, for example, by a conductor in reading a score of a new piece in a strange style, we find that it is physically impossible to scan-read an orchestral score at the speed of the music and to take in at sight all the attributes, vertical and horizontal, that the score contains. Creating this as sound in the head can only be done very slowly until an amalgam is achieved. The accuracy of such an amalgam in comparison with the real thing is difficult to test, but normal experience is that the conductor will have produced only a matrix of appropriate speeds and articulations which will then be considerably modified by the experience of the actual sound. Reading a score of a piece one has heard, or a piece in the stylistic convention of others that are well known, is a very different matter. In this case the long-term memory helps to guide the reader

I write my music away from the piano, but I have to make many alterations in my original ideas when I go to the piano and play the work through. I will add that I have spent many hours improvising at the piano, exploring for new harmonic and melodic sounds, and I regard this as a valuable exercise; but it is not composing.

Malcolm Arnold, in Schafer (1963).

Personally I use the piano because I like to. It gives one some physical compensation in an otherwise somewhat static occupation. In any case the means are not of great importance; it is the end that matters. I know of some composers who don't seem to need a piano, but perhaps they would be better if they did. It is, I feel, a help in keeping a work in check and stopping it running away with itself, so to speak, a thing which seems to happen with composers who have great facility in composing.

William Walton, in Schafer (1963).

At the examinations I was hopelessly at sea, in reality because I could not hear in my head the notes I was writing "by calculation" on the manuscript paper. I was already struck by the absurdity of having to write pastiche music away from the actual sounds of instruments or voices, let alone do composition like that. The tradition at the RCM was that one never used a piano for such work. I quickly realised that this was impossible for me. Beethoven may have been deaf, but that didn't mean everyone else had to be. I have worked with the piano ever since, keeping in direct contact with actual sounds all the time.

Tippett, M. (1991). Those Twentieth Century Blues. London: Hutchinson.

across the score, assisting them in deciding where the relevant information is and to guess at appropriate infilling. Building up such a long-term memory can be done only through considerable experience of sound in time.

It is a well-held notion in Western musical practice that composers should all achieve a state of soundless contemplation of musical structures. This kind of activity is relatively unknown in all other cultures, where instrumental performance and composition are interwoven and the stimulus of live sound is always present. The example of Mozart is regularly quoted, and there are others whose abilities and experience provide models for us. In contemporary English music Peter Maxwell Davies and John McCabe are examples of composers who work for a good deal of the time away from the direct stimulus of sound. In the case of both men the thousands of hours dedicated in their formative years to listening to and performing music and committing it to deep memory must be taken into account. Like excellence in performance, nothing "comes easy", and such a skill is acquired only after many years of practice.

Conversely there are also many composers who openly crave the stimulus of sound in what Hildesheimer, in *Mozart* (1977), calls "a treasure store that is immediate to us only when it is presented again and again". Walton was such a composer and Tippett is another. Both have acknowledged their need to hear actual sounds and to experiment with them before trying to invent new combinations and structures.

Providing sound stimulus

It is not an uncommon experience for an instrumental lesson to lack any real stimulus of musical sound. Sound is very likely to be produced, but neither teacher nor student are necessarily engaged directly with it. Rather, sound becomes the vehicle by which the problems of technique are conveyed. Many lessons consist of verbal instruction in something which cannot actually be conveyed in words. Hildesheimer (1977) again, describing this communication problem, writes: "we have to think of music as an important medium of communication. But the information, the partnership between the informant and the informed, escapes both analysis and calculation, because it conveys no semantic meaning. It cannot be translated into words, but exists and functions parallel to them, as a supplementary and yet fully fledged means of expression."

The only certain way to convey musical information is through music, and many instrumental lessons feature no sounds that are not produced by the student, making it difficult for such a student to become aware of what the good models of sound are, and making a musical dialogue between teacher and student unlikely. Again such a state of affairs is unknown in other world cultures, where the accepted teaching and learning technique is through copying the teacher. An interesting reflection on this fact is the brief report on "Music Education in India Today" by Arvind Parikh (*International Journal of Music Education*, 22, 1993), who writes: "An age-long established practice of passing on musical knowledge from the teacher to the pupil is termed 'Guru-Shiya Parampara' – the system of imparting knowledge from teacher to pupil on a 'person to person' basis. In this system great 'Ustads' or 'Pandits', i.e. acknowledged gurus or professors of music, impart knowledge to selected students with great affection and care in order to ensure that their style or 'gharana' continues." He continues by commenting that, although students now use tapes and records, "such a process can obtain only a half-baked knowledge". Even in this 'half-baked' situation the student is learning from the actual sound of music.

It has been common to find students engaged in musical tasks at examination level, and increasingly in the classes which prepare for them, where the actual experience of music is irrelevant to the task and can sometimes be considered a waste of time. Public examination boards in England and Wales over the last five years have been presented with guidelines which clearly state that, since music is sound, all tasks set in examinations should be commissioned through sound. This has fundamentally changed the national examination system and the techniques and circumstances of such examining. Personal stereo machines and keyboards, for instance, are now acknowledged as essential equipment in examination rooms. Aural tests are prepared and released on tape and the testing of breadth of historical and cultural knowledge is effected through analysis of sound recordings. Even more radically, the examination of pastiche writing including harmony and counterpoint is also bound by these guidelines; even at the more specialized and jealously guarded English and Welsh Advanced-Level examinations normally taken at the age of 18, new examining techniques are beginning to be used. There is some evidence that some higher education institutions are starting to follow this model through in their teaching and assessment assignments.

Perceiving and reacting to music as an art

The principles governing the holistic approach delineate a process which can start and finish at any point, but which, at the same time, preserves a certain hierarchy. Bennett Reimer, in his *A Philosophy of Music Education* (2/1989), suggested a very practical sequence of educational principles which work very well both for music education and outside the subject. He identified seven behaviours which were designed to increase the sensitivity of children to the power of music as an art: perceiving, reacting, producing, conceptualizing, analysing, evaluating, valuing. In this potent list we may observe the importance given to music as sound. We cannot perceive music without hearing it. The right-brain entry point is therefore maintained. By reacting we feel something at a personal level. To enhance this synthesis we do something – in his terms we produce – and this begins to engage other brain areas involving logics and analysis and physical action. Finally, through the synthesis achieved between both sides of the brain by physical action, we arrive at objective thoughts about music and subjective values.

This description of seven behaviours has never been bettered and is best remembered not as a linear sequence but as a circle enclosing the final goal of "valuing". The goal is encircled not merely because it is our final destination, but also to protect it from the teacher. Valuing needs a bastion around it since, although valuing music is the goal of all music educators, it cannot be directly taught, only taught towards. Although Reimer is careful to state that reacting involves responding to the perceived expressive qualities, his behaviours do not encourage teachers to balance right-brain procedures of creation, estimation, guessing and imagining against the left-brain procedures of analysis and decomposition. He tends to say: "now you can think, you can feel". In a fundamental way this is true, but the teacher needs to be much more aware of the processes of "feeling thinking" than that. There is a danger that his concentration on the analytical procedures of music will lead to a check-list mentality in children's approach to music. Children have to be encouraged not only to observe in detail but also to construct for themselves. Working in an art means not so much the inward matter of expressing something within you but far more finding something out there which is new to you, and finding it on your own. "Creating" and "re-creating" are the terms missing from Reimer's list.

Music is an art and must be approached and taught as an art. It is all too easy to treat it as a quasi-science, a branch of historical sociological study, aesthetics or physical education. Music education has a duty to preserve art at its centre, but this makes the teaching task more difficult. Since we all teach through the medium of language it is much easier to approach the subject through the logics and processes of language. As we have seen, although such processes figure in our understanding of music, they are only part of the story. The teaching of an art must begin and end in those areas of our understanding not reached by other subjects. Synthesis of right- and left-brain procedures through the mediation of physical action is what we aim to achieve, and since the teacher naturally finds it much more difficult to promote understanding which is not accessed through words, more effort must go into finding ways of making certain that right-brain procedures and predispositions are given their due. The starting-point and the true end of music education must always be the development of the ear.

Resumé

- When musicians talk about "the ear" they mean that part of our thinking and feeling system which deals with music. The development of the ear must be the central activity of music education.

- Teachers must place most emphasis on aural experience by involving the aural memory and appropriate actions and by resisting early involvement of left-brain notational procedures. Musical listening is a certain and distinct kind of listening very different from, for instance, speech listening. It has its own dedicated set of brain functions.

- We need to provide repeated listenings building upon earlier sound memories. Before any formal learning must come a wide experience of music as a listener and as an active participant, and we need to remember particularly the importance of the ages of eight to eleven for retaining recall of musical experience.

- Effective and multi-skilled practical musicians in our society are often those who have approached music through these first three principles.

They have learnt to play

- by absorbing enormous quantities of musical stimulus
- by letting what they hear guide them to what they want to do
- by approaching the reproduction of this music through using sensori-motor skills guided by aural acuity.

- Studying music without hearing it leads to frustration and poor practice. The sound must come before the symbol. A governing principle is: first engage the ear through action; then move to analysis through action; finally achieve synthesis through action.

- Teachers of younger children should begin to engage their pupil's attention on the inner workings of music – those elements from which it is constructed – and how these relate to style and function. A balance between listening to music sensuously and thinking about it helps to achieve that heightened awareness which synthesis between thinking and feeling can create.

- Composers only achieve working in silence away from sound sources after thousands of hours of practice. Many famous composers have never achieved this, and it does not need to be sought after as an educational principle.

- Instrumental lessons can often, quite unintentionally, centre on reading and motor skills and ignore any development of the ear or musical dialogue between teacher and student. Students often play without listening with no remedial action by the teacher.

- Most other world cultures teach music through the imitation of its sound, whereas much Western European practice tends to start from the notation.

- The enhancement of aural acuity in a lesson has to be planned carefully and a holistic approach assured.

- The teaching of an art must give as much emphasis to the creative and personal as to the logical and general.

Teaching implications

Overall principles

First plan your work and be sure what you are doing and why you are doing it. This age-old advice applies to all teachers in all subjects, and the importance of planning to music educators, both in the long and short term, has been well articulated in many recent advice documents. I can be reasonably confident in saying that the days are gone when music teachers in secondary schools made up their minds on lesson content either on the approach corridor or actually at the piano in front of the children. Questions such as "Now, 3B, what were we singing last week?" were not unknown, nor were pleas such as "I'll listen to one of your records if you'll listen to one of mine." In the primary school the equivalent has often been asked in the staff-room – "Does anyone know a song about transport to fit with my topic?" Janet Mills, in her book *Music in the Primary School* (1991), deals with this common practice

Here, I want to explore the effect of framing on music teaching, substituting for strong framing the term *instruction* and for the weak framing the more affectively charged word *encounter* …

Above all, music is a social art, where playing with and listening to others is the motivation, the experience and the learning process. This is music education by *encounter* …

Encounter and instruction correspond with the left and right of the musical spiral, with the natural ebb and flow of musical experience.

Swanwick (1988).

well, and along with Jo Glover and Steven Ward, in *Teaching Music in the Primary School* (1993), and John Stephens and Maureen Hanke, in *Silver Burdett Planning Guide* (1993), suggests helpful strategies to enable teachers to overcome this lack of perception and faulty planning.

In the university or conservatoire it is still not uncommon to find the mutual exchange of second- or third-hand information between teacher and student passing as music education. Planning at higher education level is equally important and has been enhanced more recently in some institutions by the need to justify teaching and learning strategies in detailed documents accompanying validation arrangements. There is evidence that, despite this positive move, there remain some teachers in further and higher education who consider that the onus is on the student to learn rather than on them to teach. There is certainly a strong argument for increasing student motivation and for encouraging them to take responsibility for their own learning programmes, but there is little enough help offered which enables them to do this. The aim of a good teacher in further and higher education must be to make students independent, and, paradoxically, for the majority of students this requires a very skilled teacher. The debate about the relative importance of research and particularly about what counts as research in higher education is a very lively one, but in the final analysis students are required to be in classrooms with teachers for some of their time, and it is as important for such teachers to consider how best they can help their students learn as it is for teachers in nursery, primary and secondary education.

Each music lesson should aim to be a musical experience, and this means that each lesson must contain heard music of the best quality available. Keith Swanwick, in *Music, Mind and Education* (1988), uses the term "encounter", and an encounter with music cannot happen without music being present in a context which allows it to penetrate and enliven.

Not all lessons will start directly with perceiving music. Commonly we begin a music lesson by introductory remarks, but if these remarks last too long, as they so often do, music teachers easily lose the great advantage their subject offers them – the ability to speak for itself. Teachers only have language as their main source of communication, but language is antipathetic to the musical experience and cannot contain it. We must learn to work from the music back to language, to give the musical experience preference in a lesson and to provide students with repeated hearings of examples to allow for absorption and then the processes of perception. At the same time we have to guard against passive musical experience, encouraging an unquestioning and unengaged response.

Developing the ear is based around imitation of sound and conscious analysis of it. Rote-learning is powerful and teachers must ensure that what is learnt in this way is of the best quality available. This means that the models the pupils hear must be good ones. The best models are live, and nothing can surpass the teacher as performer in voice and instrument. Live music communicates differently from and far more strongly than recorded music. The teacher's performance must, however, be good enough. A "good-enough" teacher's performance requires that it be in tune, and needs accuracy, fluency and expressive power, however simple the piece performed. This applies equally to the unaccompanied nursery rhyme as to the accompanied aria, to music for movement as to playing in and out at assembly. Realism demands that schools must also ensure that their resources of recorded music include accompanied songs suitable for children, and preferably sung by children, as well as a whole variety of listening materials from a range of genres and cultures.

The very best models are other pupils. Schools develop good singing by having a nucleus of good singers and an encouraging and good enough teacher. Positive attitudes and strong encouragement and reinforcement from the earliest age is essential in building a good nucleus of singers. Singing is a highly personal expressive act and can easily be discouraged by a chance remark. Singing a solo must be a great reward and must never be used as a punishment. School system rewards – credits, badges, marks – should be as easily obtained for good singing as for any other activity.

We learn music by imitating it, therefore at all learning stages we need to have heard enough good musical sounds to provide models for us to retain in our long-term memories. There needs to be enough repetition to allow our memories to store it. Lessons which do not contain really high-quality music will not provide good enough models for long-term development. This applies to all forms of teaching but none more so than the teaching of performing.

Teachers need to remember the parallel of learning to read music with speaking and reading. Reading the words is a process which cannot start before a considerable memory bank exists of words and constructions. Similarly, reading music should never begin until the pupils are conversant with musical sounds, procedures and constructions and can manipulate them fluently themselves.

In teaching performing we must always remember the power of imitation and that good posture, good tone and good intonation are caught from the teacher rather than taught. Instrumental lessons must be musically satisfying and the teacher should play to and together with the pupil to ensure that this happens from the very beginning. This presents a particular challenge to keyboard teachers, which they must consider. The musical memory needs to be properly stimulated through the careful reinforcing and storing of aural procedures before notation is used in place of memory.

Aural acuity is a product both of good habits in performance initiated by the teacher and of regular and careful engagement by the teacher of the pupil in analytical thinking arising from the sound stimulus. Teachers who do this well make constant reference to the intervallic constituents of the music discussed and use their singing voice as an aid to understanding.

Analytical listening is properly absorbed by pupils when the same information is central to the successful execution of a creative task. We need to avoid encouraging a passive "check-list" mentality by moving through Reimer's behaviours of perceiving, reacting, producing, conceptualizing, analysing and evaluating to activities that challenge the pupil to reinvent or confirm the rules or procedures just learnt.

Creating and re-creating need to be added to Reimer's list so that the personal response is not merely an impersonal evaluative one but a true valuing by having made something valuable. Composing/improvising is functional analysing and can best help the symbols to sound.

NOTATING MUSIC

4

Ontological parallels

In Chapter 2 I referred to the comparative study of evolutionary processes (ontology). As a teacher I have always been intrigued by the close model provided by a study of musical history in comparison with my own observations of how children learn to do musical things, particularly in the early stages of schooling. The way children learn reflects in overall terms the way we have evolved, and, in considering the thorny problem of approaches to notation, this notion of an ontological parallel together with the knowledge of left- and right-brain functions will be at the centre of my search for some guiding principles of good teaching.

From concentrating on the ear and the central part it plays in musical development, especially in the founding of right-brain skills, the focus will change to the "opposition" – the eye, through which we perceive notation. We will be concerned with reading music from symbols and writing it down. Both these processes have direct parallels in the teaching of reading and writing, and it will be important to remember a key concept from Chapter 1, of the metaphor of music as a language.

In school we can observe children recording both their own music and that of others. Guidance suggested for music in the British National Curriculum in 1992 has been particularly helpful. It asks teachers to afford opportunities for children to discover their own musical notation through experiment and it also requires teachers to provide experience of many forms of notation, cues and signs.

The teaching parallel here is in the experiments with writing words that young children undertake before they learn to copy letters, words and phrases exactly. Some teachers actively encourage what is known as "emergent writing" and look for the shapes of letters and words beginning to form in scribbles that are full of meaning for the children who make them. For some years now this has been useful practice in some British schools, and it has been possible to observe how many individual children approach similar work in music. We now know some of those ways in which children commonly approach the problem and can understand some of the tricks and pitfalls. In following through the parallel with writing, it is obvious that before writing must come reading and before reading must come expressive speaking, except in very extraordinary circumstances.

The ontological correlation between what children do now and the experience of earlier people in notating their music is fascinating. Bob Samples, in his book *The Metaphoric Mind* (1976), explains ontology:

*Biologists, embryologists, and paleontologists use a phrase that in a sense is one of the more metaphoric statements in science. **Ontogeny recapitulates***

Children's development of tonal harmonic concepts roughly parallels the evolution of harmonic thinking in Western art music.

Peacock, D. (1994). "Stages in the development of tonal thinking", British Journal of Music Education, 11, July.

The symbolic metaphor exists whenever a symbol, either abstract or visual, is substituted for some object, process or condition. The abstract category – letters, numbers – is processed by left brain. The visual category – logos, road signs, mapping – is right brain.

Samples (1976).

Children should … record their compositions using symbols where appropriate.

SCAA (1994). Music in the National Curriculum: Draft Proposals.

Freud says: "Thinking in images (*Bildern*) is only a very incomplete form of becoming conscious. It is somehow nearer to the unconscious processes than is thinking in words, and is older than the latter, both ontogenetically and phylogenetically." "Image" (*imago*) is meant here not as "picture" (*tabula*) but as an independently arising representation used as means of reproduction and communication. Only through a willful creative act does the *imago* become a *tabula* (or *pictura*), sublimated into an artwork. Although this activity is a conscious process, capturing the vision in the artist's product, it does not include conceptual thought. It is rare to find a thinker among painters; even the greatest were less seekers in the abstract than finders in the concrete. Even the inventors among them, the Renaissance artists, were guided less by conceptual speculation than by a drive for knowledge, less by a world view than by an ideal of innovation, if only a technical one. "Thinking in music," on the other hand, is explicable neither ontogenetically nor phylogenetically. On the one hand it is further from verbal thought than is thinking in images, since it begins without conceptual, and certainly without material, content; on the other hand, its transposition into a creative act demands not only a craft much more complex than that of all the other disciplines but also a dimension of thought *sui generis*. This is the conceptualization of its future realization, i.e., its performance, the process through time of that which the composer has drafted as something static onto the paper before him. Thinking in musical tones is an anticipation of their eventual event.

Hildesheimer (1977).

phylogeny. The egg develops in a way that is parallel to the way the species has evolved from more primitive forms.

"Ontogeny" means the entire sequence of events involved in the development of an individual organism, and "phylogeny" means the entire sequence of events involved in the evolution of a genus or species. For the purposes of this study, our "organism" is notation and the "genus" is music. To provide evidence for this ontological correlation it will be necessary for me briefly to sketch out the principles of the evolution of working music notations in as much detail as is known. We need also to think a little about what connects the visual and the aural processes in inventing sounds and symbols for them.

Music and early man

The need to make marks is one of the oldest human impulses. It has been argued by psychologists and anthropologists that this mark-making represents the most fundamental leap forward in the evolution of intelligence. As far as we know, the first marks were pictures and emanated straight from stimulation of the right brain. This fundamental leap forward is wonderfully documented on the walls of caves in Southern France and Spain. It was expressed not as written language but as a formalized visual representation in shape, colour, texture and tone. The images represented the important aspects of the world in which those people lived. It is unthinkable that such mark-makers were not also able both to make and control sound. The ontology of the process of human development now gives us a clear pointer to the existence of music in the mark-makers well before these wonderful marks were made on the cave walls, since the two areas develop early in our growing brains.

Musical memory is one the earliest mind processes to develop – older indeed than mark-making. Children of a few weeks old can store and receive complex sounds in musical form. It has been shown that they can remember and react to remembered melodies. Ontologically speaking, the ear and its connected musical brain processes must equally have played a vital part in the first human development. On a purely utilitarian level these processes would have assisted in the hunting of animals and birds. One of the most ancient of instruments which is still played in the form in which it was first invented is the Chinese xun. This egg-shaped fired-clay bottle has been found by archeologists in sites of New Stone Age dwellings from 7000 years ago. The earliest examples had one hole as well as the blowing hole, and it is thought that these were used to reproduce the mating calls of birds and animals. (By using our clasped hands and blowing through our thumbs we can produce a similar though more unreliable and primitive sound.) It is our misfortune that no concrete evidence remains of the musical techniques used on this instrument. Perhaps those first superb paintings of animals also had a function as mnemonics for associated melodic calls? Making pictures about the music you have just invented is a commonly found practice in children of four, five and six.

First musical mark-making

Humans first started to make marks which we are certain represented musical sounds somewhere around the time of the Warring States

(5th–3rd century BC). Little enough is known in the West of ancient Chinese culture and traditions, but it is recognized that some of the oldest surviving examples of musical notation come from China. The distinction between notation for musical sounds and that for words or names is unclear and the two often merge. Pictographs or pictograms are pictures or symbols standing for words or groups of words. They can also just as easily stand for musical sounds and groups of sounds.

Such Egyptian wall paintings and carvings of music that exist use pictographs, often showing in detail the musician playing the instrument in different poses. Indeed, what is recorded is not so much exactly what was played but the fact that it actually took place. A parallel in children's work can be found in those many first drawings and paintings of themselves or others doing something.

Early music notation in Europe

The writing down of music in early times came partly from the need to preserve what otherwise would be lost. Rather as the Romano-British buried treasure to avoid it falling into the hands of the marauding Saxon invaders, so priests or musicians given charge of the musical traditions of worship had to find a way of preserving the melodies for their sacred chants. The method of recording had to be proof against the fragility of human life. What was recorded was the fruit of many hundreds of years of tradition. In each case what has been preserved earliest is what was considered to be essential. Inessentials or givens were omitted. Examples can be found in the early Indian Rig Veda chants and in the Ancient Greek Hymn to Apollo. In all cases of early music writing, what is conserved is what can most easily be forgotten. What is not conserved is that which is either easily construed or unimportant. Writing music down was also a powerful method of control in a world where communication was difficult and the power of church leaders had to operate over vast distances. Some of the earliest records of books of music are in the volumes of chants chained to the altar of St Peter's in Rome.

Two forms of early music notation commonly existed. The first stemmed from the singing voice and the second from the playing of instruments. Both these notations are currently in use today. Vocal melodies when associated with words are most easily remembered, especially when they are in rhythmic lines and contain rhyming devices. The recording of the words alone is generally enough to activate the musical memory of the melody. If the melody became complex then the most usual device employed was that of sung words, or "vocables", associated with degrees of whichever scale was being used. This ancient practice can still be found in India, where the vocables sa, re, ga, ma, pa, dha, ni, sa are utilized, corresponding roughly to the ascending degrees of our familiar Western scale. Dhrupad singers use these syllables to sing incredibly fast melodic lines where the pitch is clearly matched by the vocable. The singing of the vocable becomes part of the artistic experience.

Similarly the ancient Chinese tradition of naming provides the vocables gung, shang, jiao, zhi, yü for the five main notes of the major pentatonic scale, with chin-jiao and bien-gung as intermediaries on the subdominant and leading note. Modern Chinese practice has relegated

The first humans to make marks were thus *literally* marking a gigantic leap in the evolution of world intelligence, for they were externalising the first traces of the mental world. In doing so, they were fixing their thoughts in time and space, and also enabling their thoughts to span those same dimensions. Human intelligence could now communicate with itself across the infinite reaches of time and space.

Buzan (1989).

Recognition of pictures is essentially perfect. The capacity of recognition memory for pictures is almost limitless.

Buzan (1989).

Eastward from Babylonia, in South india, chanters of the Veda use a similar script (similar to that found by Villoteau (1798–1801) in Egypt and learned from the Ethiopian priests): syllables, like *ka, ki, ko* and other consonant-vowel combinations, indicating groups of notes, not single notes, are inserted in the text or, as in Babylonia, written by the side of the verses. Not only is the Veda cantillation very old, but this form of syllabic script is expressly called the oldest Veda notation.

Sachs (1943).

Melody followed ready-made patterns or was composed of carefully classified motifs, not of single notes. As a consequence, notation developed in the direction of group scripts, accents, and neumes, not of pitch scripts.

Sachs (1943).

A remarkable example is the musical notation invented in the island of Bali by learned Hindu-Javanese who in the sixteenth century AD had escaped from the Mohammedan conquest of their native Java and wished to preserve their traditional music from oblivion in a new country without tradition. It consisted in a kind of shorthand: the five notes *dang, ding, dung, dèng, dong* were simply rendered by the little symbols for the vowels *a, i, u, è, o*, without indicating rhythm.

Sachs (1943).

Sarah Glover (1786–1867) lived and worked in Norwich. She reused ideas of Guidonian Solmization, gleaned largely from J. J. Rousseau's articles on music in Diderot's *Encylopédie*, and applied them to the teaching of psalms to a children's choir. She made particular use of the modular, a chart with the Sol-fa terms written on it, to which she could point. She had a glockenspiel made for her in glass and silk thread by the local blacksmith, and used this as pitch reference in her classes. It was the effectiveness of her work plus that of Wilhelm in Paris that so impressed Hullah, who recommended it through the inspectorial system to schools nationally. A collection of Glover's books and associated artefacts are now kept at the Strangers' Hall Museum, Norwich.

these ancient vocables to the realm of theory, where they are used as scale and key references only. Instead the Western system of Sol-fa, combined with a numerical system for rhythm, is currently used by folk musicians to record music.

Notating using the singing voice

Modern European practice in vocables is founded on a six-pitch system first invented by Guido d'Arezzo, an eleventh-century Italian monk, and the vocables ut, re, mi, fa, sol, la first derived from the opening syllables of each line of the words to the Hymn to St John the Baptist *Ut queant laxis*. This medieval system was well known and used by scholars and teachers, and it was recorded in many reference texts, including the influential *Encylopédie* of Diderot. The French substituted "Doh" for "ut" since it eased performance for singers.

Sol-fa was taken up by English music educationalists such as Sarah Glover and John Curwen in the nineteenth century and had considerable effect on early British music education. Some teachers still subscribe to the traditional practice, especially in isolated pockets in Wales and Scotland. The absorption of this system by Zoltan Kodály in Hungary earlier in the twentieth century, allied with a Hungarian government specialist music school system, has given a new lease of life to Sol-fa as a method. One of the great practical advantages of such a scheme as notation is that it provides a sounding system which can be written down using the alphabet and it can also easily be typeset. The French system of solfège uses the same theory but fixes Doh as C. French children using pitched-percussion instruments with solfège marking are therefore more easily able to notate their invented or remembered melodies in solfège. Children who have been taught Sol-fa should be encouraged to write melodies down as words without reference to an instrument, thus avoiding the problem of the fixed location of Doh.

Young children think in concrete terms and need to have a one-to-one relationship with what they are doing and how they are thinking about it. Interconnected abstract thought requiring the transposition or modulation of gestalt is a property of a much later stage of development of the brain. Notating melodies using Sol-fa syllables not only best enables young children to write down invented melodies directly, it constantly reinforces for them the sound and progression of the main scalic patterns. It also provides an easy musical logic. The teaching of this requires two things of teachers: first that they teach their young children the Sol-fa vocables; second, that, if the children use instruments as aids to invention, they mark pitched-percussion instruments with Sol-fa syllables. Sol-fa encourages the building up of strong comparative relationships between the tonic (Doh) and the other degrees of the scale. For this it draws upon and reinforces the right brain, particularly when the improvised melody is sung. Sol-fa developed its rhythmic side in the nineteenth century based on commonly found typographic punctuation marks. Although it is reasonably efficient for simple music, it is not now commonly used and leaves the system somewhat one-sided, dealing only with the storage of pitch.

The theory of tonality and a movable key structure is one that is initially difficult to grasp, and the majority of British primary school teachers will be unable to explain it. Knowing that, whatever pitch you start on, you can construct its matching musical scale can be assisted by early Sol-fa learning, but many teachers, not having known the system themselves, can find it merely an annoyance. Sol-fa appears to them to be just another parallel system imposed on top of the eight-letter alphabetic one of which they have some knowledge that is confirmed by the instruments available. Sol-fa, however, is equally well known to musicians in many parts of the world, not only in its various culturally diverse forms but as it stands. Many folk and classical musicians use Sol-fa as reference. It is taught extensively in China and Japan and in many parts of the USA. Some American states insist that all music education texts used in the state have Sol-fa references, and it has been shown to be of great assistance in developing aural acuity in music. Teachers are highly recommended to use the system, especially with young children.

Like all systems it has its limitations. Sol-fa does not easily adapt to anything but simple scalic melodies. It is possible to develop it into major and minor scales or modes, but this requires a good deal of mental gymnastics and begins to impose a complex parallel system on one which is already quite complex enough. Knowing that Doh is the home note, and being able to memorize the intervallic relationship of the other degrees of the scale to it, is the essential basic information. This can be taught by all teachers who are willing to sing with their children and who provide opportunities for melodic invention. The famous Richard Rodgers song from *The Sound of Music* is a great gift to teachers, however hackneyed it may seem to adults. Its derivation in the play is, after all, from a governess who teaches music to her charges, and it is a system the real Maria von Trapp herself knew and used well.

Notating using instruments

Some of the earliest surviving fragments of notation from Ancient Greece are based on the playing of the lyre. What is preserved is a system of numbers and symbols representing strings and finger positions on the strings. In the Renaissance a very detailed notation for the lute and other plucked string instruments was developed using similar principles. This is called tablature, and the famous Elizabethan songwriter John Dowland was expert in its use.

Today a quick glance at any sheet music of popular songs or folk melodies is likely to provide evidence of similar devices still in operation. Beginner guitarists are often provided with a tablature or diagram of string and finger positions, and as they become familiar with these hand shapes they are formalized into a written symbol using letters. The majority of popular songs published have guitar chord letters written at the appropriate point of change. Little is done to show the rhythm played, since this will be improvised appropriately, although beginner's books sometimes show how many "strums to a bar" by a series of oblique lines.

This treatment of rhythm lies neatly within the ontological parallel, since in all the known examples of early notation the pitch has always been the thing it was considered necessary to record. Obviously this was because the pitch was found to be more difficult to memorize, whereas the rhythm came directly from the associated words.

Much of children's early experimental improvising and notating will arise from playing instruments – mainly percussion. From the nursery

Many early directive notations were teaching aids rather than instructions to the performer – directions, that is, at second hand. In one point, however, all notations from earliest beginnings almost to the present day find common ground. Durations, timbre, inflection, mode of attack, may or may not be specified by the notational directive at different times and places. But all notations have been concerned to specify pitch, or the relationship of pitches.

Cole (1974)

Monks had, as early as the ninth century, devised a notation in which the letters of the alphabet from A to G represented a C-major scale. It was only later that it was shifted in order to start from the modern note A, which was the lowest note of the lowest church mode. Guido d'Arezzo, the greatest theoretician of the eleventh century, has been credited also with devising the perfect staff notation that we have used to this day, though we have added a fifth line. The original four lines and the three spaces in between them housed seven consecutive notes of the diatonic scale: the first, third, fifth and seventh notes were privileged with places on the lines, while the second, fourth and sixth were squeezed into the intermediate spaces. The abnormal consequence – so hard to grasp when you try to learn music – is that, of two notes an octave apart, which carry the same name, one is allowed to perch on a line, and the other is not. And the same is true of notes a fourth apart.

Sachs (1943).

The main systems can be listed as:

1) Alphabetic notations, using words, syllables, or letters to stand for single sounds of fixed pitch
2) Directional signs, to indicate rising or falling pitch
3) Group signs, to indicate melodicles – recurring groups of notes that always appear in a set form
4) Tablatures: action notations which lead the player's fingers to the required place on his instrument.

Cole (1974).

school years on, individual children will find ways of preserving their musical ideas in written form. One of the most commonly found systems used by children is pictographic notation. Often the instrument to be played is drawn, sometimes in great detail. Earliest concrete thinking will provide a result which requires the child to draw the picture of the instrument every time it is played. Four beats on a tambourine will produce a line of four carefully drawn tambourines. Sometimes pictures will be drawn on the same piece of paper which are the equivalent of titles. An improvisation about dinosaurs can, for instance, be specially decorated with a picture of a dinosaur alongside the pictographic notation. To the child these two pictorial methods will seem equally important, the one representing the actual progression of sounds, the other how the music feels.

Some children will spend a laborious amount of time drawing out diagrams or pictures of instruments and marking in on them the appropriate place to play a single note. A group of ten-year-olds produced some such effort for me recently. They finished up with a large sheet of paper covered with meticulous tablature diagrams of a glockenspiel. Each diagram was identical, but on each a different bar was coloured in, indicating the pitch to be played. The rhythm was left to their memories, reinforcing the ontological principle. We only need to notate what we otherwise would not remember. Despite their rather clumsy first attempt, they were indeed repeating some of the basics of early instrumental notation. Children tend to do what earlier people did.

Children who have experience of staff notation in their class via the teacher or through music experience outside the school will often wish to use the shapes of staff notation in their efforts to record what they want to communicate. The more naturally teachers refer to staff notation in their daily teaching the more likely it is that children will make their first musical notation in a similar fashion. It is one thing to use the shapes in a playful way, and quite another to begin to use the logics of the system. It is unlikely that children below the age of seven should ever want or need directly to use staff notation as a system, but they can benefit by becoming familiar with the shapes through play and other activities.

When the exploration of pitch is assisted by pitched-percussion, the task is made mechanically easier for the older child to notate what they have just invented, but there are pitfalls. These instruments are universally marked with the European letter system of fixed pitch. Children naturally use the letter system as a way of notating since it also uses the familiar alphabet. Unfortunately it utilizes the alphabet in a way which does not easily make sense to children. The logic of why the most commonly used scale starts on C and not on A is bound up in the historical mess into which European music notation has grown and does not help children to understand the basics of music theory.

There are a bewildering number of types of music notation still in use worldwide, including pictographic, heightened word script, letter notation, tablature, Sol-fa, staff notation, numbers, chord symbols in letters and numbers, graphic, graphs, and the electronic/magnetic pulse which is the basis of all recordings.

Interconnectedness of artistic function

The impulse of early man to record music as pictures emphasizes for us the interconnectedness of artistic function in many early and present cultures. In turn it also reflects the complex interrelatedness of the structures of the right hemisphere of the brain, about which very little still is known. The modern French composer Olivier Messiaen, for instance, described how he had a visual experience of music which allowed him to see chords in varying colours. This became a principle of his composing method, and he referred in his writings to the way that certain drugs can provide a similar effect by easing the pathways between areas of the right brain. Coloured, linear, textural and spatial associations with musical sounds are not uncommon human experiences and derive from the internal structures of the right brain.

The ability to experience a crossing over between two or more aesthetic areas, or synaesthesia, is a known phenomenon, but is not experienced by most of us under normal conditions. However, it is not unusual, for instance, for musicians to connect certain key centres with specific colours or textures. The development of music for the theatre and then the cinema and television, and indeed the development of opera, bears witness to the need we all share to relate between aesthetic areas. Children will naturally use both colour and shape in recording their music, and this should be encouraged. Their earliest attempts at recording music which is processed by the right brain also emanate from adjacent procedures in the right brain.

Interrelated artistic skills

Musicians in many emergent cultures were and are people who had and have many other aesthetic skills indistinguishable from music. Skills in literature, dance and visual arts were, and are, often found in one person alongside the healing arts and sciences. This also applied to musicians in our Dark Ages and medieval period. The minstrel, jongleur or goliard was also an all-round entertainer. The English folk singer was traditionally a ballad writer as well as a melody maker and performer, and the Welsh bardic tradition, in both its eighteenth-century form and in its more ancient form, looked for a cohesive relationship between poetry and music. The harp in legend, fable and history is accredited with the virtue of healing powers. The troubadors and trouvères of medieval France were equally concerned with poetry and music, as were both the Minnesingers and Meistersingers of Germany. The links between music and poetry may seem opposed laterally, since it is the left brain which controls speech and the right brain which receives and decodes musical impulses. As we have seen, though, the workings of the brain, are not at all simple. In poetry and lyrics the meanings of words are only part, indeed a small part, of the poetic function. The pure sound of words and their network of implied and metaphoric meanings are even more important. Sound and metaphor are both apprehended by the right brain, and we can begin to grasp some of the complexity of interrelationships which go to make up aesthetic understanding. The appreciation of poetry draws upon both hemispheres and, according to the style of poetry, may well draw upon the right brain more strongly than the left despite poetry's medium being words. Perhaps one of the distinguishing factors of poetry from prose relates to which half of our brains we most engage in perceiving and understanding it.

Interrelatedness of art forms as a cultural norm

The interrelationship of art forms has some physiological basis in the way we process our perceptions of them. Most particularly in our ability to understand metaphor we are enabled to translate an impulse from one aesthetic area to another. In the modern world the Balinese language still has no single word for music, since the experience of music in that culture is firmly integrated with allied arts. In many cultures dance is so well integrated with music that the two are inseparable. The drumming traditions of various parts of Central and West Africa interact with dance, costume and ritual. Many Indian dance traditions have a common factor in the intimate inter-relationship of body movement and the sounds which go with them. The Brazilian Carnival combines dance, music and applied visual arts. Japanese Kabuki, Noh drama, Native American dancing and Chinese Peking opera all share a similar interaction between the arts. In our own Western culture we can still witness survivals of this kind of close relationship in formal ballet and in social dancing of all types. The contemporary "disco" has a triple meaning of a place, the sound and the movement. The English Morris dancer knows a sequence of dance steps by name, and with that name will be associated a melody and a given speed as well as other routines and costume.

Specialization and the enhancing of notation's role

Whereas it was the norm in our early Western culture for arts to interact firmly, increasing sophistication has led to increased specialization within any chosen area of practice and with it a parallel isolation of brain function. The narrow gets narrower. It was not until the end of the eighteenth century in Europe that the notion within the practice of music of the specialist composer as distinct from an all-round practising musician came into being. Specialization was enhanced by the individualistic philosophy of the Heroic and Romantic movements and by the growing trend towards individualism.

The notion and practice of a composer who only writes music and who does not perform it lead quickly to an enhancement of the role played by notation. Over the nineteenth century, European composers became increasingly remote from the actual performance of their music and risked losing contact with both the performers and the audience. No longer did the performance of complex pieces still contain a random element of improvisation. By the end of the nineteenth century notation was dominant in the composition process and improvisation had largely become a lost art. Music was transformed, in computer terminology, into what-you-see-is-what-you-get. We can find examples of the ultimate enhancement of the role of notation in European and American music in the mid-twentieth century when the marks made on the page were used as stimulus to the invention of musical sounds. John Cage's searching-out of imperfections in the music manuscript paper to decide on the pitch positions of notes and Bussotti's huge visually stimulating graphic scores both give examples of the eye leading the ear.

Many other contemporary musicians working in high art areas specialize, and the working model of the practice of the composer has for a long time been that of someone writing things down. There is a modern notion that the very best practice of composing is in isolation and in silence, committing to paper what is heard within the head. However, in other fields of music, practice differs.

Notation and vernacular musicians

Folk artists, rock musicians and all those whose musical expression is in "common musical speech", or the musical vernacular, rarely specialize only in the writing of lyrics or music; at the same time they are also performers and advanced technologists. Their working practice is largely through improvisation and also sometimes arises from interaction with others. The re-emergence of the multi-skilled musician has come about through the explosion of vernacular music all over the world, fuelled by economic pressure. This sort of musician – the most common type of musician in today's society – tends not to use traditional staff musical notation. The reasons why vernacular musicians reject notation are complex, and to some extent derive from a purposeful dismissal by such people of traditional classical values and practice. In doing so they are unconsciously returning to a much older and more commonly human model of practice. One prevailing reason for this rejection is that staff notation is unnecessary to them and inadequate for their purpose.

Although the tape recorder and, more recently, the computer are the main recording mediums, notes and jottings are made to aid the memory, and from the observation of what is actually written down by such musicians today we can learn much about what is essential in notating their kind of music. From observation of such practice we can begin to sense a principle in music education which suggests that musicians notate what they need, when they need it and in the most convenient form. Indeed, this was the basis of figured bass in the Baroque. Need is the key word, and teachers must bear this basic principle in mind.

The problems of putting notation first

It is not uncommon to find that a child (and possibly the teacher) has interpreted the task of inventing a piece of music on a pitched-percussion instrument as the random playing of pitches and their recording. It is easy for teachers and children to set off down a very unmusical path through taking this cognitive approach to a musical task. With the insistence in British schools that all children compose, there is increasing incidence of this problem. Teachers, themselves inexperienced in music, also tackle the problem using a cognitive strategy. The reasoning process is as follows: "I have to write down some music, well, let's make some musical sounds and write them down as we make them. That way I will not forget which sounds I have chosen." Well-motivated children of five or six can spend a great deal of time playing a chime-bar, noting down its name, then playing the next one, producing in the end a long string of letters. When the child comes to play this back to the teacher it does so laboriously by reading each letter in turn before locating it as a chime-bar and playing it. Unfortunately the task has become reversed in its learning principle, since the need to notate has overtaken the impetus to create sounds. If teachers have understood the parallel with reading and writing, in this case they would have encouraged musical expression to develop securely first and, having done so, only then considered the recording process.

Similarly there is a real danger of using an atomized approach to music notation, the equivalent in reading being the teaching of individual letters or words in isolation. Some teachers have found a kind of instant success in isolating simple rhythm patterns with children of eight or nine. The notation is presented in flash card form with rhythm isolated from pitch, therefore without heads on the notes or staff lines. The equivalent in reading terms would have been the rather doomed Initial Teaching Alphabet, whereby word shapes were simplified, making for easier recognition. The lesson proceeds by the class clapping and using agreed mnemonics when the flash cards are presented in various orders. A composing task is initiated by limiting the choice to combinations of the two and then playing or clapping back the combinations. As can be seen, this approach is from the symbol to the sound and focuses on logics and analysis of pattern, not really advantaging any musical decision or experience through right-brain intuition or sound-pattern making. It approaches a composing task as a notational puzzle.

Although this provides an accessible lesson for non-skilled teachers, since it is almost entirely left-brain oriented, it by-passes the musical experience almost altogether and can produce a "barking at print" response from the children which leaves them with almost nowhere to go afterwards, since no real musical skill has been involved.

Terminology of notation

Children need rational and systematic use of technical language throughout their schooling. We have already been through a confusing change from imperial to metric measuring systems; indeed, we are still in a somewhat confusing transitional stage, to be experienced every time we shop or buy fuel. Music has its own particular problems of terminology. Linked with the visual symbols of staff and other notations is the problem of commonly understood terms. Perhaps it is not surprising to find Britain out of step with most of the rest of the world, using its own fanciful set of historic terminology whose logics reflect truly the land of Lewis Carroll.

Whereas most of the Western world, logically, uses fractional names for each measurement of time, Britain and those countries affected by its practice – Australasia, for instance – does not. Instead we use a motley collection of terms. Whereas in Europe the standard time division is known as a "quarter note", we use the term "crotchet". This word means "crook" or "hook", and is an ancient French term derived from medieval monastic practice describing the actual look of a written symbol of a stem with a hook on the end. Stems with hooks on the end we call "quavers", which is an English Renaissance term for "shake" or "trill". Further divisions add on prefixes, producing the ludicrous "hemi-demi-semi-quaver" for the smallest note used. The European "64th" is so much more rational and efficient. Similarly, as the British go up the scale of values, so the names actually suggest a diminishing to any linguist. What in Europe is a "half-note", in Britain is a "minim", despite its being one of the longer notes. The European "whole note" is a "semi-breve" in British terminology, using the French word "brève" meaning "short". We also glory in the longest normally used note, found mainly in church music, and known, of course, as a "breve". Just to confuse, the longest note possible, and rarely seen, is called a "long".

What we call a "bar", Europeans call a "measure", which is accurate. The "bar" is actually a printing term for that vertical line dividing one measure from another, which we British have to distinguish by adding a word and calling it a "bar-line". Europeans use the term "metre" to describe the division of pulse into sets of two, three, etc. We use the looser word "time" and talk of "two time" or "two in a bar", which has a friendly ring, but "metre in two, three", etc., is more accurate.

More confusing is the difference between the words "tone" and "note". The word "tone" already had two common British uses in music, one to describe an exact measurement of a step of pitch of two semi-tones, and one to describe the quality of sound made by an instrument. Since the mass sales of Japanese- and American-made machinery in this country, we now commonly use the European term "tone" to mean a pitched sound, as in "Please speak after the tone" or "two-toned door bell", because the Americans use the rational European term brought to America by early European immigrants and the Japanese learn American English.

Beethoven and Mozart were used to distinguishing between "tone" and "note" (*Ton* and *Note*). Tones were heard and notes were written. It would, again, be far less confusing if the British also adopted the European system. One common confusion is that many students write about the "twelve-tone *scale*" of Schoenberg, making parallels with the whole-tone scale used by Debussy. The Schoenberg example should translate as "twelve pitch series", avoiding the structural confusion, since Debussy's scale is exactly measured in equal intervals of a tone, but it doesn't trip off the tongue too well. We also speak of "tone-colour", whereas the German equivalent is more accurately "sound-colours" (*Klangfarben*), producing an interesting cross-art use of the word "colours". The National Curriculum recommends the nineteenth-century French term "timbre", which derives from the Greek for "drum" – but this sits uncomfortably on the British tongue and teachers are often unsure whether to use a Churchillian anglicization – "timber" – or to grapple gamefully with the French "i" and "r". "Sound quality" seems simplest in this case.

However charmingly eccentric most of these pretty English terms are, there is no way that they can be at all meaningful to children except by rote-learning, and it will be to our future professional musicians' considerable disadvantage if our schools continue exclusively to promulgate this practice. We need rational and internationally reputable terminology throughout our education system. The simplest thing for teachers to do for the time being is to use both systems of terminology, rather as we still do at the filling station with gallons and litres. Eventually, and sad as it seems to me, it would be best for British music educators to use European terminology throughout and let the old terms gradually become a decorative part of our heritage industry, along with rods, poles and perches, farthings, shillings and half-crowns.

Targets of attainment in notation

Our system of primary and secondary schools provides a natural break somewhere around the age of eleven, and this yields a useful watershed for notation teaching. In the primary phase before eleven it is important for teachers to concentrate on building up first the musical equivalent of expressive speech – singing, improvising, playing – and regularly and naturally using the materials of music. Until children are fluent in these behaviours it is completely unnecessary and probably harmful to encourage them to write anything down using formal systems. Just as you need to talk before you write, so natural musical expression must be firmly established first. Children only need to write something when they know what it is they wish to write and have it firmly in their memories.

Children learn to read as the next stage after learning to speak, and reading musical notation can be built up in two ways – firstly as "scan-reading", as in "to glance over quickly". This means becoming familiar with the shapes and patterns made for familiar songs and melodies, and can be done by having these around the classroom, referring to them and by taking parts of them and placing them on flash cards to use in conjunction with the music. Children of older primary age can become skilled in scan-reading songs and lines of the melodies of listening examples.

Secondly, children can learn to perform from notation, the equivalent being reading aloud with exact expression and timing. It is salutary to remember how long it takes for children to attain this level of confidence in actual reading and to consider how much background work has produced this over how many years. Children can learn to perform simple phrases that they have first memorized using the notation of those phrases as aids to their memory, and most children of primary age play from notation by a slow process of memorization. The actual task of playing an instrument and reading notation from a book at some distance from the player is one of considerable difficulty, and in some cases is well-nigh impossible. Any teacher who can easily sight-read music accurately at speed playing a school xylophone or glockenspiel, hitting the right bars each time and avoiding the wooden case, has appreciable skill.

Secondary phase schools have the main task of involving pupils in learning to use the notations necessary to their tasks. Those schools using keyboards will inevitably need to teach standard notation, but the principle of sound before symbol must still be maintained. Secondary teachers should never allow the task of writing notation to become divorced from the musical context. The need to write something down must be there, otherwise the motivation to learn will not arise. The notation that is best suited to the purpose is the only sensible one to use, but it will be important for all pupils to have a purposeful experience of standard notation.

Musical tasks have to be created for pupils to ensure that, to complete them, standard notation must be used. A continuing strong experience of notation as central to the performing task and good availability of progressively complex scanning material should advance learning of notation on all fronts in an essential musical way.

Resumé

- There is a useful correlation between how man has learnt to notate and how children learn the same task. This is known as ontological observation.

- We know that musical memory has the potential to develop in the womb. We also know that early man made wonderful paintings, the function of which is still not understood. Paintings and musical sound emanate from the right brain. Very early instruments are known about, and it may be that there is a connection between the paintings and musical sounds.

- The first musical symbols were invented to preserve that which might be lost. Two early forms of notation dominated, the first from the practice of singing and the second from that of playing.

- In Western culture, notation using the singing voice was the first to develop. Pictographic notation was employed in early civilizations and is used naturally by children today when they wish to explore ways of recording what they have invented.

- Tablature is still commonly used, as is its condensed version, chord symbols. Children often choose to record only pitch, and this can be done through use of tablature diagrams of the instrument. We record only what we need and are likely to forget. Letter systems are often used by children and untutored adults to record their melodies. Letters are also used to record chords.

- Synaesthesia is very strong in some emergent cultures now, and is likely to have been strong in early man. When we make symbols for sounds we need to draw on skills across two areas. In medieval and Renaissance days there was a more common interaction between words and music and visual art than at present.

- As we in the West have become more sophisticated we have also become more specialized. Specialization, particularly of composer and performer, has thrown an extra emphasis on the use of notation, and improvisation has ceased to become common practice. By the same process the sound can become separated from its symbol.

- Musicians working in the musical vernacular use only what they need and mostly ignore standard notation.

- Many children in infant classes have already encountered the shapes of staff notation and teachers can use flash cards with phrases on them to highlight key motifs in the music. The parallel with reading technique is strong here.

- Teachers involved in encouraging and facilitating the act of writing with young children can apply the same measures to the recording of young children's music, forgetting that the experience in creating music is much smaller in most children than that of language. There is also a danger of approaching notation in an atomized fashion, taking phrases and symbols out of their context and creating simplified systems. The lack of any following through and the lack of stimulus to the musical imagination tends to leave children frustrated by useless learning.

- It is important to use musical terminology rationally and logically. Primary schools should be concerned mainly with the establishment of familiarity with standard notation through scan-reading and performing. Writing music down should be encouraged only when it is necessary to the completion of a task. Children should be encouraged to find their own methods of notation.

- Secondary teachers will need a careful strategy for the introduction of reading and writing notation based on real musical experience. Alongside studying standard notation, pupils should be encouraged to use that notation which best suits their purpose.

Teaching implications

Example 1

When working with an individual child of about six years old, the teacher helps the child first to establish by experiment a pattern of pitches that are pleasing to the ear and memorable. This can be done merely by suggestion and allowing the child to experiment on their own, or through interaction, asking "How about this pattern? Or this? Now you make one for me." The child then must be encouraged to repeat what they choose by playing and possibly by singing the pattern several times, thereby helping their musical memory to retain the pattern. There is no need for children to notate anything at the first attempt at making a new piece of music; they should rely on their memories.

Only when several patterns are well retained as linked information making a memorable piece of music should any notation be attempted. Notation can be as the child decides. Most often the child will wish to write down the letter name of the relevant bar, but they could use colours for each pitch, shapes, patterns, etc. Some children will laboriously draw a picture of the instrument for every pitch played. The notation is then used as an *aide-mémoire* for performance, and the child is encouraged to rely mostly on their memory and looking at the instrument. The notation is mounted and displayed by the teacher.

Example 2

The class of six-year-olds has learnt the "Divali Song" (see Appendix) as part of their work on Divali. During a "hall" time (a time-tabled slot allowing use of a larger space than a normal classroom), their teacher gets them to sing the refrain "Brave Prince Rama comes", and asks them exactly how many notes there are in this refrain. Having ascertained that there are five and having asked the children to count them on their fingers as they sing, the teacher then asks the children how many different pitches there are in that same phrase. If necessary, the teacher demonstrates by stretching out three fingers horizontally and, with the other hand, pointing to the shape of the phrase. The children learn to imitate this and to find the shape of this melodic phrase, which begins on the middle pitch, repeats, moves down one, jumps over to the top, and returns to the middle.

Next the teacher reels out some masking tape, makes a line on the floor and repeats the exercise by stepping on the line, beneath it, above it or across it. Children are invited individually to do the same. Next the teacher makes available the three chime-bars of the pitches used in the refrain (D, E, F) and these are placed at the end of the line, with the E centrally placed at the end of the taped line, the D below it and the F above it. The children can decide which direction should be up or down. Pairs of children are asked to come out and one plays the melody while the other steps the refrain along the line.

The whole song can be built up in this manner, with the opening phrase being learnt next and the middle phrase last. All the other chime-bars necessary are added (G, A, B, C).

Finally the children are encouraged to play a pair game where one plays a melody and the other steps it, or vice versa.

Example 3 (over a short module of a few weeks)

A class of ten-year-olds is studying map-making in their class. They have made maps of their locality and of their school. From discussion with the teacher the children reinforce the elements of map-making, talking about colours, lines, symbols, words and scale. The teacher then explains to the class that they are going to make a different kind of map today – one of a piece of music. The music chosen is a short excerpt from "Max's Sea Journey" from Oliver Knussen's *Where the Wild Things Are*, although the piece is not identified by the teacher. The music is first listened to all the way through, the children having been told to make a note of any facts they can obtain by listening. A discussion follows and the teacher amasses information on the board. Things such as instrumentation, dynamics and length are accepted as facts about the music. The music is played several times more while the children begin to understand better what is asked of them. Opinions and analogies are deflected or rejected, since they are not factual.

Next the class is asked to listen again and this time individually to draw on paper the equivalent of any musical shapes they hear. The teacher offers to play the music in short sections with a pause between each to allow for drawing time, repeating where necessary. At this point the teacher reveals the source and title of the music and some discussion takes place. The next part of the session helps the children to order the musical shapes in sequence, either from left to right or from bottom to top, etc. The class is asked to think of the progress of the music as a journey from one place to another, with events on the journey. As on a map, they can start their journey from any given place to any other.

Various maps are created and after discussion about the virtues of each, matched against listening again, a group of children is commissioned to make a large wall frieze of the same subject.

Another group (or groups) is set the task of creating their own musical journey, this time from a specification given by the teacher. One such journey is described in a worksheet written by the teacher based on a journey from home to school. The children must improvise and then record their musical equivalent of this journey as a map. They may also produce a written description of their improvisation and the process by which it was produced.

Another group is set the task of writing in words a detailed description of the music they have heard, using their drawings and notes as reference. They are encouraged to use both factual information and analogy, including also personal opinion.

All the work is mounted and displayed for a time as a music project.

Example 4

Ten bars of the opening of the Bourrée and eight bars of the opening of the Minuet from Handel's *Water Music* are prepared by the teacher, either on sheets or overhead slide. The teacher explains that the class of nine-year-olds will be listening for repeating shapes and asks them to listen carefully to hear if they can distinguish any. The class is not listening to what instruments are playing or what the music suggests to them, and this is explained. There will be two playings. The teacher then plays the relevant bars of the Bourrée twice and a discussion ensues, about repeated shapes. Some children may notice rhythmic shapes and some pitch shapes in the patterns they hear. They may notice larger formal repetitions. Next the relevant piece of notation is made available and the excerpt is played again, with the class being asked to answer the same question with the aid of the notation. A further discussion ensues, which could get into some detail if the lines and spaces between pairs of pitches are counted and then that interval between two pitches is looked for elsewhere. Shapes that are inverted can also be distinguished. If a worksheet is available the pupils can draw rings and numbers or colours around pairs of like shapes. The same procedure is repeated with the Minuet.

Example 5

Using the taped recording of the song and accompaniment of David Eddleman's "I Don't Mind", and making the notation available, the teacher teaches the song to the class of ten-year-olds (see Appendix). The first melody is sung by a man, the second by children. In the refrain the melodies are sung together. The class is asked to listen to the song and to follow it in the notation by tracing the progression of the melody with their finger. At the end the teacher initiates a discussion about where the finger trace went during the refrain, and some decision is made about which line should be followed as the class listens again. The teacher encourages those who can join in to do so. As they approach the refrain, the teacher warns, "Watch out for your line!" The next part of the lesson concentrates on learning melody 1 and melody 2, trying them out and fixing them in the children's musical memories as strongly as possible through repetition, either with or without the tape. When the class is secure enough to be divided into melody 1 and melody 2, two teams are chosen by the children based on the strongest singers. As they sing in their teams the teacher emphasizes that they should tap each note as they sing it and remember carefully which line they take when they get to the refrain. This needs doing more than once for success. When the class is very secure in singing their parts the session is extended, maybe at another time, by the teams learning the other's part and reversing the roles. Performances then can be arranged where the teams alternate parts by repeating the song. Finally the class is challenged to trace their parts by tapping each note as they sing their melody, and when they come to the refrain to tap the notation of the other team's part while they sing theirs. This can be practised by using the tape and just listening and tapping the page.

Example 6

The teacher prepares a set of flash cards with the chord symbols G, D7 and C on one side and the Roman figures I, V7 and IV on the other. The class is given the notation of "John Barleycorn" (see Appendix) and the song is taught using the taped recording of the melody and accompaniment as a support. A group of children is given access to pitched instruments that allow them to play all or some of the notes of the chords on the flash cards (G, B, D; D, F sharp, A, C; C, E, G). The lesson proceeds by alternating children on the task of singing the song or playing the chords. The teacher holds up the flash cards, letter sign outwards, on the cues given in the notation. Individual children are asked to take charge of this job. The flash cards can, at some stage, be reversed, showing the Roman signs, and this can similarly be practised. The class is then set the challenge of working out what these numerals mean, the teacher giving the essential clue that Roman I is G. The Roman numerals may also need to be taught as a separate exercise. Each group of the class is given an opportunity to play the chords in time with the song. The number of groups will depend upon the availability of instruments.

Example 7

A class of 12-year-olds has worked on the idea of sequences, repetition and inversion in melodies. They are given the notation of Larry Eisman's "If I Were You" (see Appendix) on a worksheet and asked to work in pairs at keyboards, playing the melody and finding ways of filling in the blank bars based on the motif of the first bar. Alternatively, the task can be done by discussion, with pupils coming out and writing on the board or overhead slide. Either way the melody's progression should be decided by hearing what is there and improvising what should come next, either on keyboards/instruments or by singing. The completed song is performed by the class. The class is asked to look carefully at the finished result and to find examples of repetition and inversion.

Commentary

There are many different sorts of notation beyond the standard Western system. Graphic symbols and colours can be used very freely, pictures can be drawn, diagrams, numbers, letters, etc. We use notation as an aid to our musical memories, to add extra information as we listen, known as scan-reading, to perform music from and in order to write music down when we invent it. Each example lesson focuses on a different use of notation. In Example 1 of composing writing, the teacher is careful to encourage the child to invent a melody and to "fix" it in the memory before any notation is attempted. The right brain is given full focus first before left-brain procedures are explored. The "reading" of the final notation is done by combining both, but emphasizing right-brain memory of shape and sound. This way the musical shapes or patterns will always be guided by the right brain's ability to hold such shapes and interlink them with others. The principle of ear first, followed then by action and lastly by eye, is here maintained. Notation should be brought into play only when what is to be notated is firmly formed and committed to the memory.

This sort of individual work is obviously at a premium, and it is difficult for teachers to find time for music when they need it all for reading, number and science. However, ancillary helpers and musical parents can be enlisted for just this kind of task, and there are likely to be spin-off advantages in coordination and general development, since music is such good schooling for the brain.

Example 2 shows how movement learning can be well combined with first steps in notating. If the whole song is mapped out then three lines will be needed on the floor, built up one after the other, when the children discover that they are necessary. This method of introducing children to the principles of the stave is very good for sorting out the conceptual differences between lines and spaces, since many children feel that it is illogical to write over the line, and cannot understand how a line can equal a space. It approaches notation through movement, aural memory and spatial conception, thus engaging right-brain energy with some help from the left.

Example 3 makes certain that the music is listened to for shape and pattern, enhancing the right-brain focus and giving each child a defined task in interpreting these shapes as graphic symbols. As the lesson proceeds towards more detailed analysis, the musical memory is strengthened by repetition and left-brain logics are increasingly being drawn in, balancing the right-brain graphic symbols and colours that can be used. Some of the follow-up tasks explore the link with words, which increases left-brain involvement. Personal comments are asked for and individual appraisal is therefore built up.

Example 4 again concentrates on listening for shapes and patterns but this time uses the notation as a guide. The patterns are sought first only through listening, giving advantage to the right brain, but left-brain devices are also brought into play through the use of notation. This lesson is an example of scan-reading of notation. The notation is not used as a performing cue but as a visual cue to enhance listening.

Example 5 shows notation being used in performing mode, although it is approached through scan-reading first. As the lesson progresses the children's attention is increasingly focused on the notation and how it can help the memory. The final challenge, achievable only by the most adept in the class, is to read two lines at once, or at least to memorize one line and point to another. It is this kind of fluency in reading that we should be looking for at this stage in the most adept pupils.

Example 6 uses three forms of notation at once, chord symbols and standard notation all in performing mode. The chord symbols are given in two versions commonly found, making the third form of notation. The Roman numerals link with key, and the final task explores this link, involving left-brain logical and computational procedures.

Example 7 shows notation being used in a very restricted, "closed" composing mode task. The notation is also used to identify other devices. Although this lesson is very much a left-brain lesson, the little progressions implied by the melody given are very strong and emanate from right-brain patterning. The class is encouraged to play or sing through the answers rather than invent them through left-brain visual or computational logic.

Teaching Composing

The principles already discovered in previous chapters will continue to inform the following analysis of the principles of good practice in teaching composing: establishing aural memory and forming aural concepts before any symbolization is attempted and then making certain that the symbols and the sound interact in the head; approaching musical tasks as whole-brain activity promoting action; and using ontological principles as a guide to developing practice. Since the act of composing is firmly associated in many people's minds with the actual writing down of musical symbols, the first principle, that of forming aural concepts in the head – sometimes called internalization – must be particularly carefully encouraged by good teaching strategies. The process of composition is essentially an isolated act and we do not yet have a wealth of recorded evidence of good practice. Only a few composers have attempted to define their processes of composition for us or have provided any detailed record of their own teaching.

Britten once described the composing process as like approaching a house in a mist. He explained that first you could discern its overall shape and that it was only when you were very near to it that you could begin to make out some of the details. Using right-brain techniques to imagine music in the head first, not in detail, but in large overall shapes, is an important technique to be established early in young composers. It is noticeable that Britten does not suggest that he knows all the details of the music before he writes it. Rather the act of composition, of writing something down, is like opening the door and actually exploring the house. It is the overall and holistic concept that comes first, and this kind of initial right-brain thinking process needs to be respected, encouraged and nurtured by teachers.

There are also descriptions of Britten's lessons as a young boy of 13 or so with Frank Bridge, which throw a good deal of light on the purposeful quality of the development of Britten's musical imagination and memory – his musical ear – by his teacher.

Bridge's method was to take pieces that Benjamin had written since their last meeting and go through them on the piano. "I used to get sent to the other side of the room. Bridge would play what I'd written and demand if it was what I'd really meant." In a 1960 interview, Britten recalled how "Bridge used to perform the most terrible operations on the music I would rather confidently show him. He would play every passage slowly on the piano and say, 'Now listen to this – is this what you meant?' And of course I would start defending it, but then one would realize ... as he went on playing this passage over and over again – that one hadn't really thought enough about it. And he really taught me to take as much trouble as I possibly could over every passage, over every progression, over every line."

Britten gradually realised that there were two "cardinal principles" in Bridge's

I begin first by becoming aware of the overall length of the work, then of how it will divide itself into sections (perhaps movements), and then of the kind of texture or instruments that will perform it. I prefer not to look for the actual notes of the composition until this process has gone as far as possible. Finally the notes appear ...

Michael Tippett, in Schafer (1963).

A complete human consciousness involves the polarity and integration of the two modes as a complete day includes day and night ... The process of building a house provides another example. At first, there may be a sudden inspiration of the gestalt of the finished house, but this image must be brought to completion slowly, by linear methods, by plans and contracts, and then by the actual construction, sequentially, piece by piece.

Ornstein, R. E. (1977). The Psychology of Consciousness. 2nd edn, New York: Harcourt Brace.

The fear of being wrong seems to be the prime inhibitor of the creative process and this phobia can be traced back to the earliest influences. Emphasis on correctnesss, on right and wrong, black and white, true and false, deals a lethal blow to independence and imagination.

Ferguson (1973).

Findings provide evidence for the role of the right hemisphere in processing emotional information.

Bryden, M. et al. (1982). "A left-ear advantage for identifying the emotional quality of tonal sequences", Neuropsychologia, 20.

Recently Robert Saxton, Head of Composition at the Guildhall School of Music and Drama, London, said in interview with a student of mine (1994): "Britten advised me not always to think of the notes first, but to try to imagine the colours and shapes of the music first".

Results suggest that the anterior-right hemisphere may be critical in the processing of pitch components in music; the right hemisphere in general may be important in maintaining the internal auditory representation of musical material, essential for detecting violations in performance.

Shapiro, B. et al. (1981). "Selective musical processing deficits in brain damaged populations", Neuropsychologia, 19.

teaching. "One was that you should find yourself and be true to what you found. The other – obviously connected with the first – was his scrupulous attention to good technique, the business of saying clearly what was in one's mind."

Carpenter, H. (1992). *Benjamin Britten: a Biography*. London: Faber & Faber.

In the light of some of the principles of good music education emerging from this enquiry, we can understand what Britten describes very clearly in terms of brain process plus some essential teaching communication skills. Without doubt Britten was an exceptional pupil; however, what even he needed most was the attention and respect of the teacher, which is a first-base communication skill. First Bridge accepted that whatever Britten brought him was worth his time and attention, and this is perhaps the teacher's most important priority in forming an effective teaching strategy in this difficult creative area. My observation is that all composition pupils feel desperately exposed in bringing their first efforts for scrutiny. There appears to be something far more personal and fragile in sketches for musical composition than even in those for poems, books or paintings and drawings. I cannot rationalize this easily, but, having taught composing for many years at secondary and undergraduate level, I have found that inevitably the first remark a student makes in a tutorial is an apology for the quality of their work. Composers feel dreadfully unsure about their own efforts perhaps because of the speculative element in all musical composition. Composition pupils respond very quickly to the teacher's willingness in the tutorial to give what they have done serious thought and attention. A chance negative remark, however, can send them plummeting down, and teachers need to be most careful to approach any negatives through positive strategies, especially in the early stages.

The description of Bridge's insistence that Britten sat on the other side of the room is also interesting, since this relocation must have done two things in particular. First it denied Britten the ability to use his eyes to reinforce his musical memory, since the more usual position in a tutorial is for the pupil to sit beside the teacher so that both can see the manuscript. This forced the whole process back into an almost exclusively right-brain dominated thought process for the pupil, throwing him back to his initial motivators in creating the music that largely emanate from the right brain.

The left brain must be in operation but the right brain holds the upper hand. The teacher played back the music very slowly to the pupil, which removed some of its intuitive and emotional effect and exposed more clearly its underlying structures, enhancing analytical left-brain thinking. It is likely that Bridge played his own variants of Britten's detail, challenging his pupil to determine what it was he actually imagined before he wrote it. Asking a pupil to justify what they have done, in words, at a distance from the keyboard, increases this partnership of left- and right-brain work, demanding the most difficult task possible – that of describing in words a process that has no verbal equivalence.

Some of Britten's answers to his teacher (and we will never know exactly what these were) will have been given in terms of technique – where an obvious mistake had been made in, for example, the balance of a chord or texture – but some of the answers can only have been made in metaphorical terms, taking the composer right back to the initial motivating factor of the piece in question.

This movement backwards and forwards between right- and left-brain processes, while always giving the advantage to the right brain through focused attention on sound, intuitive thought and holistic planning of many kinds, provides us with the best model for the composition teacher. The process of composition can best be understood as a spiral, into which teachers interlock their teaching process, activating new initiatives of thought and action. The function of the composition teacher is not so much to suggest a particular outcome as to identify where change needs to be made.

I was taught composition at university by Humphrey Proctor-Gregg, who had been a pupil of Stanford and who had adopted many of his teacher's mannerisms. The same process of playing back slowly was used, and he did convey respect for what I brought him, although often in a somewhat patronizing manner. The relocation of pupil and teacher was not used, however. In contrast my lessons with Alexander Goehr and Jonathan Harvey all took place in a situation where no sound or notions about sound were shared between pupil and teacher. These lessons were at adult level, and perhaps it was assumed (wrongly in my case) that the inner ear was completely and satisfactorily in operation in both teacher and pupil, leaving no need for sound actually to be used. However, in both these cases the lessons maintained an intellectual level that stimulated argument in the world of ideas but did not challenge basic musical technique. The exchange between teacher and pupil was not based on heard musical information and was exclusively left brained.

The only one of my teachers who managed to operate successfully in a whole-brain manner was Hans Keller, who spent most of the lessons talking in detail about the harmonic and rhythmic structures I used. Despite the fact that he rarely had recourse to playing the keyboard, he managed somehow to convey the sound of the music through conversation, technical discourse and gesture, with the occasional hum and whistle. I went away from these lessons, which usually took place outside in his garden, always with a greater feeling of self-worth and of renewed purpose in artistic expression through composing, and an enhanced aural awareness of my own music.

The composing process starts from an intuitive base but moves quickly on into areas of logic and linear development. As these proceed there needs to be a constant reference back to the holistic conception, checking and balancing, as new pieces of technical detail become reality. The final arbiter of success is in the right brain's intuition and affective response, since this was also the initiator, and the process of assessment mirrors this.

Initial right-brain thought processes use intuition, perception of sound, holistic conception and shape forming (gestalt), and can be excitingly if tantalizingly vague. This excitement is brought about through tension, perhaps caused by the contemplation of the rift between the possible and the realizable. The tension is not the sort that wears us down, but it is rather more akin to that which can elate us. The initiating processes of a work of art, however minor it may be, are elating to the creator,

It is the metaphoric mind which causes us to build cathedrals – and the cathedrals are built with rational logical plans.

Samples (1976).

Findings indicate that affective responses toward previously heard stimuli were more favorable and judgments were more positive when the stimuli for processing were presented in the left rather than the right hemisphere. Data support a cognitive-affective model in which affective responses are the last step in a series of cognitive processes over hypotheses suggesting that affective responses do not depend on prior cognitions.

Anand, P. et al. (1988). "The cognitive-affective model versus the independence hypothesis", Journal of Consumer Research [Columbia University], 15, December.

The left brain houses ordering of linear time, secondary access to cultural metaphors, and the filters that screen, organize and systematize experience into "reality". The right cerebral hemisphere contains processing of cyclical time, primary access to natural metaphors, and the freedom to reinstate all of the twenty or more natural senses in the presence of the natural reality.

Samples (1976).

The role of rhythm may be central to the creative process. Since the alpha rhythm has been implicated as a possible timing device for the brain's mathematical transformation of stimuli into sensory data, perhaps psychology will investigate the data-processing uses of bio-feedback and the related altered states. The most creative individuals are in an altered state much of the time.

Tension is certainly a component of the creative process, but it should be compared with pleasurable excitement, such as sexual arousal, rather than crippling anxiety.

A sense of urgency is also present – a state of fear that unless the idea is worked upon it will be lost.

Ferguson (1973).

Initially a young composer will rely on a superficial understanding of the forms of his culture to determine his goal. As he grows he begins to determine more fundamental principles which underlie particular forms. Detailed study of Bach and the contrapuntal masters has traditionally been set for young composers. From this immersion one gains essential familiarity with the potentials and possibilities of the tonal medium. A lot depends on what is stored in the long-term memory.

Sloboda (1985).

and it is this feeling that is nearest to what has been called inspiration, which literally means an intake of breath, and that draws us back again and again to the often painful process of creation.

The practice of composing proceeds through constant interaction between the two opposed brain hemispheres, where the left brain provides us with ability to produce detail and to record it with accuracy, and the right brain monitors and considers the effect of the detail upon the whole. The teacher must be able to engage in this process on behalf of the pupil and act as a good conscience on their behalf. This, indeed, is what Britten describes Bridge as doing. Having accepted Britten's work as being interesting, having slowed it down, thus making it more open to left-brain analysis, Bridge demands whether this is what was meant, forcing him back to his original motivations and challenging his musical memory.

The teaching of composing has sometimes been dismissed as impossible by otherwise eminent teachers. Many composers themselves refuse to teach, and in our society we lack the opportunity of working alongside other composers in workshop situations. Composing has not been an everyday experience or a normal activity in our society. Specialization has exalted the role of the some composers in Western society so much that many of them appear to have become remote from and insensitive to society's needs, intent only on leading or forming taste and not reacting to it. The more composing becomes a remote and specialized task the more it is inclined to become left-brain oriented, reliant on notation or, for some now, computer-stored information. There are, however, many working composers who produce music to order, or modified by the varied demands of concert programme, theatre, film, television or dance. Such composers need to be multi-skilled and to be able to work in any style, and teachers must bear this firmly in mind.

In vernacular musicians of this kind we still have a strong tradition of the composer-performer-technician – someone who invents, plays and records as appropriate – and this model is far more likely to influence young composers in education than its classical equivalent. Such a predominantly right-brained approach based on sound and musical memory should be encouraged by teachers since it provides the most potent foundation for all future skills. The matter of musical style is largely immaterial except in the sense that pupils need to have a wide experience of styles. Although pupils may well be engaged in arranging and producing parodies or pastiches, as they may be in literature studies or art, their own individual creative work can only stem from the musical language with which they feel comfortable. Although this will vary according to the social and home environment, the majority of pupils from about the age of ten or so will choose to express themselves in the vernacular, currently rhythm and blues, reggae, soul and ballad.

The choice of appropriate materials and projects in composing for each age-group is one of the most challenging problems facing any music curriculum planner. Class-based teachers and specialist teachers working with young children have to be able to provide a learning environment in the classroom where composing tasks, both individual and group, can take place. They most need to have faith in and rely on children's innate ability to create and their wish to do so. Specialist teachers of older children, however, should be conversant with a multiplicity of styles and also need to be creative in them themselves in order to enlarge their older pupils' musical horizons through activities and projects. The guiding principles in designing composing activities are of appropriateness to the age-range through task, content, conceptual difficulty, manipulative skill, feeling response and working practices. Style in individual compositions should normally be the choice of the pupil.

Composing is not an easy discipline and it draws upon skills of prediction and analysis not commonly used in other areas of our lives. Composers can be compared with architects, but they also need to be well trained as builders. The technical disciplines, experienced through sound, cannot be side-stepped, and teachers must plan input of technical know-how and experience throughout a child's school life. Just as for creative writing in language, the teacher must provide much stimulus, including many models of good practice, as well as building knowledge of available techniques and the opportunity to practise them. For teachers dealing with pupils taking their first steps in composing, it is most important to remember their need for the musical experience, retained in the memory to precede the recording process.

Alongside the principles revealed to us through brain research, I have identified those that stem from ontological observation, and it is important also to see whether there is yet enough experience of the way our children compose to compare it with how societies have evolved composing practices.

Encouraging children to compose within the education process is not such a new thing. The amazing work of Satis N. Coleman in New York in the early 1900s presents us with excellently documented information on the composition process in very young children. Much evidence collected by music educators working with very young children shows that the most natural form of early musical discourse is that of song, interacting words and music. The single line of melody, it can be argued, is the basis of all composition, and this can be traced through clear evidence in all cultures.

For all that is known of the development of music in our culture, and that of other world cultures, the single melodic line forms the essential strategic base. Voices come before instruments and the inner expressive urge to compose is most naturally expressed through the voice. The need to tell stories and to heighten their expression through music is universal. The earliest music to be recorded was song, from Ancient China and Ancient Greece to the Vedic hymns of India and the chant of the early Christian Church. In each case the single melodic line was recorded first only in pitch, leaving the rhythm to the memory and the prompting of the word rhythms.

We do not know whether Satis N. Coleman's pupils actually recorded their music or whether it was only written down by their teacher, but observation of children in our schools clearly shows that the ontological parallel is, indeed, present. Children naturally improvise song and, when left, or encouraged, to conserve and record their music, will record only the pitch and general presentation of shape and structure. Precise rhythm is left to the memory or word rhythms.

Some artists have unintentionally perpetuated the myth that technique is unimportant. A university music teacher complained that many accomplished pianists misled aspiring youngsters by telling them that it is only necessary to "image" the way the music should sound. "They've forgotten that they had long ago acquired the technique that makes it possible for them to perform spontaneously now."

Ferguson (1973).

Men vent great passions by breaking into song, as we observe in the most grief-stricken and the most joyful.

Vico, Giambattista (1725). The New Science, lix.

All passionate language does of itself become musical – with a finer music than the mere accent; the speech of a man even in zealous anger becomes a chant, a song.

Thomas Carlyle, quoted in Chatwin (1987).

Historically, Western rhythmic, or mensural, notation developed several centuries after that of pitch notation, and it is the only system to have become precisely detailed in this area. Its development appears to have been prompted by several factors. One was the need for logical theory to underpin practice, as church music became increasingly complex through use and experiment. By far the most effective spur to the invention of mensural systems was the increasing use of instruments in the performance of art music. Once the melodic line was divorced from words, it became important for performers to have a clearer idea of how their parts fitted in with the rest. Pitch only was insufficient.

So, through observation of composing practice, we find a reversal of a very common music education principle – that of teaching rhythm first divorced from pitch. Children left to themselves will ignore the recording of what they perceive as intuitive rhythmic elements in any detail, finding them unnecessary. Hours of my time as a child were spent in frustration at the back of a class, shaking jingle sticks in a percussion band, and never being given the drum I longed for. The percussion band charts from which I played were logical and clear, and as a six-year-old I could sight-read from them with some skill. By the age of 13, when I first needed to write down music of my own, I still found myself unable to record, systematically, the simple rhythm of the hymn I had written. Years of experience as a teacher has shown me that, however deceptively simple rhythmic notation appears in performance, the concepts needed to use it accurately as a writer are very hard won. Pupils of upper secondary age often find it easy enough to record the pitch they need, and even the harmonies, but struggle to find the correct metrical and mensural equivalence. Accurate recording of pitch can always be checked against an instrument, and is therefore mostly right brain in operation, but that for rhythm depends on an abstract conceptual process which draws heavily upon left-brain procedures.

We have to be able to isolate the rhythmic motif to be recorded, if necessary slow it down to detect the lowest common-denominator of pulse, before analysing the constituent parts and building up the rational symbols. The recording of pitch without reference to an instrument is a high-level skill, slow to develop in those without perfect pitch, and right brain in derivation but left brain in analysis. It is linked strongly with vocal improvisation in early childhood. The underlying principle of whole-brain thinking being the ultimate goal is once more demonstrated.

Working practices

Since composing in a large class had no derivation in any teaching experience before the 1960s, working practices are only just beginning to form. There has been a tendency for work in secondary schools to follow John Paynter's Schools' Council Project model and to divide classes into sub-groups for the purposes of improvisation and composition. In primary schools, where composing work has taken place, it has been almost totally based on group work. This is fine in the upper primary age-group where children can work socially, but produces many problems with younger children. Teachers have to manoeuvre carefully from overall educational principles governing how children can work best.

There is, and always will be, a place for the teacher-directed lesson, even in this highly personal and creative area. Not only do techniques need to be taught, but teachers acting as improvisers or composers themselves are likely to be the most powerful stimulus to the children to undertake the activity themselves. Composing has to become a normal activity in the classroom involving both teacher and pupil. In the final analysis composing is an individual act and, in the pragmatic organization forced upon teachers by large numbers of children and limited equipment, it is very easy to forget the need to encourage and stimulate individual work.

Working with individual young children

Songs and stories

The basic structural and expressive unit of music is the song. Stories are articulated in words and as such could appear to be left-brain material. However, the expressive nature of a story is not to be found in the concrete meaning of the words but in the structure of the story and in the significant relationships between characters and events that the story conveys, which are perceived and understood by the right brain. The combination of logical sense and sequence with imaginative insight and large structural purpose binds together opposing brain functions and provides that unique perspective on life to be found in stories.

A song is also a kind of story, and the structure of music, even when not a song, is directly related to the story structure. Perhaps it is pertinent that our language (and other related languages) provides no equivalent word for a piece of music which is not a song. We talk about "a piece" and then have to refer to the genre, such as quartet, dance, sonata, concerto and so on. This lack of terminology is particularly experienced in the conversational use of musical terminology in our society today. Many of us refer to any piece of music as a "song" whether it is instrumental or not, especially those whose musical vernacular is commercially processed music based on blues and rock. If the word song is not used then the referent is "track" or even "album", which is merely the recording device. The basic structure of all Western European popular music is the song.

Songs are potentially stories and become stories by extension. Ballads function as stories, and the epic poems from the beginning of our cultural records were also songs. We name them interchangeably so that a chanson or lay, ballad or aubade are both stories and songs. When we begin to work with children as teachers and to guide and encourage their first adventuring steps in creating their own music, this interrelationship of song and story can help to provide essential signposts. The most difficult part of musical creation for the child (and for any beginning composer) is finding a way of sustaining an idea, of spinning it out over time. Song and story structure are most helpful in underpinning this.

An objection made by some music educators to the linking of story and musical invention is that this will encourage children, and therefore adults, always to perceive music as representing something. This certainly is a danger, and adults can be very distracted by such biased early learning. Such critics of this way of involving of children with programme music prefer to encourage a more abstract approach, concentrating on listening to the materials or constructional elements of the music, and to eschew what they see as a "Mickey Mouse" approach.

In my experience, children like to do both. No one could deny the tremendous power of the story in music and song, and its polymath development, opera, would not function if it were not so. Neither would music in film and television. Inevitably children will want to express concrete images in musical form, but they also have an inbuilt understanding of the expressive purpose of musical materials themselves. For instance, they respond to a melody in its own right. The "up-and-downness" and the "going-alongness" of that melody is in itself expressive, and the sensitive teacher will be able to inspire and encourage both perceptions in their children. The teaching of techniques, elements and structures can happily exist alongside the telling of stories in music and the invention of songs. The important thing is for the teacher to recognize which is which and when and how to encourage the interaction between the fixed and the concrete and the analogous and the intuitive.

In creating music the young beginner usually approaches the task through the left brain by a process of describing and naming. For instance, "Let's make a sound representation of something we know: a thunderstorm. First we need to think of the sound of rain, thunder, etc." The child then proceeds as nearly as they can to match each sound with its nearest symbol. Although it will be obvious that a banged drum really sounds very little like real thunder, the left brain will accept it readily as a reasonable symbol: a sounding symbol. In the same way, a child accepts the matchstick man he or she has drawn as a human figure, and very often labels it too – or the adult does.

This allies itself with the concrete level of thinking in young children proposed and documented by Piaget. Concrete musical thinking produces one-to-one matching of stimulus and response. All young children respond readily to the task of creating sound pictures in this concrete, one-to-one way. "Here's a cow, let's go 'moo'. Here's a train, let's go 'chuff-chuff, woo-woo'." In many children's early life this type of concrete response is initiated and reinforced strongly by parental or adult stimulation through reading. "What sound does the dog make?" is a common question asked of very young children in their first two years. The response is usually approved of highly by the adult, especially since that adult very likely fed in the response in the first place. To find the direct results of their own teaching coming back to them so strongly is pleasing to the adult, and the child soon accepts and takes part in this game. In fact the accompanying question is most probably unnecessary, since "What sound does the dog make?" as a meaningful sentence may well be beyond a very young child's comprehension. However, the combination of the expressive inflection in the adult's voice, the accompanying gesture and sometimes a picture clue all coalesce into a signal which says to the child, "This person wants you to do something. Last time, this sound pleased them. Have a go, you can't lose."

It is interesting to note how many young children play this game with adults without ever having heard the stimulus sounds in reality. The most obvious clue to this is the train, which still appears to sound like an American steam train of the beginning of the century. The adult has passed on to the child a handy sound symbol and the child responds. It is unsurprising therefore that many first experiments in sound by children draw upon such ready-made symbolism just as they do in drawing and painting. In fact it is more likely that a child will come to school with a ready-made set of sound symbols than with a similar set of drawn symbols. The success of "Old Macdonald" is in part accounted for here. The next move on will be to chain these sounds together as groups or sequences of sound information. Some versions of "Old Macdonald" do this in the refrain, stringing together a growing sequence of sounds. An excellent foundation skill exercise in composing is for the child to make up new sequences.

The Swanwick–Tillman research (1986) suggests that children's earliest sound explorations will be limited by the shape and construction of the sound resources used. For example, a child playing a school xylophone will usually produce sliding sounds across the bars as well as random beating on them. Often the box is as interesting in sound as the actual bars. Purpose-made musical instruments are not the only things which make interesting sounds. Melodic improvising with the voice is, of course, far more fundamental, and is not subject to shape and construction. There is a concerning tendency for adults to encourage in children the notion that composing means banging something. In other words, the child must go to an instrument to find its first experiments. In later stages of development this becomes an increasingly acute problem and could well be one of the source problems in retarding the development of composing. As soon as we stop relying on our inner voice and our imagination and "let our fingers do the walking", a new set of psychological constructs begin to take over and the eye begins to control the ear.

A basic technique in exploring sound with a child is that of repetition. The child is invited to make a sound pattern and the adult repeats it back to the child and then the child back to the adult. This can be done with very small children. The praise which comes with this action is the forceful motivator for learning. Clear rhythmic patterns can be "stored" in this way, as can children's exploration of dynamics – tapping very quietly, for instance – and tone colour – trying out different materials, such as wood, metal or glass. A sensitive adult working with a very small child can encourage constructive exploration and also impose necessary limits for the health and safety of both. We do this in providing painting activities for very young children by stopping the paint brush going into the mouth, for instance. Learning how far you can go to make a good sound on a tumbler with a spoon is important. Also it is necessary for the child, with the adult's help, to find out how to make a range of pleasurable sounds which do not threaten destruction in any way either to the artefact or to the hearing mechanism.

It is more likely that adults will have noticed, encouraged and even preserved early mark-making of children that they have acted similarly

Culturally we tend to distinguish visual sensibility, which we all share at some level (children's drawings and Leonardo's are linked somehow), from musical sensibility, which we regard as special (children's banging on the table or vocalising are not seen as linked to Beethoven or even to Madonna).

Waters (1994).

on sound-pattern-making. Beyond this hurdle placed by adult perception an added difficulty is to be found in preserving the sound-patterns the children invent. When children in class sing or play spontaneously there are strategies a teacher can use. The first is simply to feedback and reinforce by sensitive comment. Just, "That's nice, John", may well be enough. A follow-up comment on the increasing quality of his voice and seizing on the positive things – finishing on the tonal point, for instance – will add to the reinforcement of the activity. Such reinforcement can be done by the teacher, with some subtlety, maybe joining in with the last few notes of a phrase of the cadence, or imitating back to the child with some comment such as, "I liked the bit that went …" The best thing is for the teacher to ask for it again and to see if the child can repeat it. It doesn't matter if they can't or don't, but the musical memory is being fully exercised in trying.

It is not difficult for a teacher to create opportunities for pupils individually to explore the making of drawn or painted symbols. But it is technically more demanding of the teacher to provide a similar opportunity in sound. In both arts areas the exploration and establishment of personal symbols is a vital part of learning. Providing a conducive environment in a busy classroom where such work can go on with individuals is a problem, but a good deal of ground work can be done in teacher-directed large-group activities combined with singing. Versions of the game "I went to market and in my basket I put …" can be played using sounds instead of words.

There is a further problem in that the limit of one-to-one sound experiences is fairly small. Compared with the world of shapes and colours in which we live, the sound world we inhabit is limited. We can sensitize our pupils to all the sounds around us – insects, birds, machines, people, air – but as soon as we stop to listen to these sounds in our classrooms we can be far more aware of the large expanse of silence which surrounds them. In contrast, observing how many shades of blue or even grey there are in a sky through the classroom window is an almost endless task, and the matching of these in pigment, dye or coloured paper calls for great perception and skill. Learning to listen acutely is important, but it will not necessarily help a child to make the requisite first steps to musical composition in quite the same way that children can learn to look.

It is the songs we sing for ourselves inside our heads which are most important. We have to learn to "listen" to those sounds which we have constructed in our imagination, and this is an advanced skill which takes a major step beyond the direct stimulus of the heard thing. Many adults have never had this experience. The parallel experience in drawing and painting is a fascinating one, since most adults view such activities as directly concrete in experience. They engage their analytical thinking process. The object is selected and recorded well or badly. But this is not what very young children do either in painting and drawing or in music. They start in all of these fields from a different point: from the inner experience. The very young painter's brush is not directed by any kind of brain activity that says, "A tree doesn't look like that", or "My mummy has a blue dress with pink spots." They do what they feel at the time and the expression comes out straight from their inner world; at least that is what it seems like to us adults. It is only as young children begin to develop that the need to represent and try to capture the real world becomes so important for them. This is about the same time that they begin to want to match sound with symbol. Adult reinforcement added to their own need to come to terms with the concrete world forces concrete thinking upon them in the arts and begins the long trek away from the source. In some ways one can view the whole of arts education as a cyclic process of trying to get back to that source, that intimate connection between feeling and doing that we had as very young children, while being able to behave and respond as adults.

A dilemma of early musical invention is that, when the task is most stimulated by the focus of an imaginative inducement, with the intention of capturing the child's intuitive power (right brain), the composing child most commonly turns to the concrete naming area (left brain) to complete that task. We cannot be surprised at this since it is a natural state of affairs in our society and culture. Children quickly learn that this is what society wants them to do. Left-brain activities always get the best rewards. Most societies are so deeply committed to, if not highly biased towards, left-brain thinking that a child can go right through formal education with little or no stimulus for or development of the right brain at all. The more "formal" the schooling is, the more likely this is to be so.

With somewhat older children in the upper infant and junior school, the art educator approaches the problem of encouraging whole-brain thinking by helping children to observe things clearly enough to draw them, seeing them as they are rather than as they think they might be. The music educator working with the same age-level has a rather more complicated problem, for there are fewer models to imitate, nothing much to hear as it really is. A beginning can be made in the infant school by carefully considered imitation – dried peas on a tray, for instance, in imitation of rain on a roof. This can increase the sharpness of focus of children's listening skills, which is a virtue in itself. Sensitivity to and analysis of sound is a foundation music skill. But this kind of thing has not much relevance to simple real musical experience. Music just doesn't sound like that except in the most sophisticated abstract examples. By the time children get to school the process of musical enculturation is already well established. They know what music sounds like and what it doesn't sound like and they have already begun to form prejudices for certain systems of musical communication.

Melody, the most direct expression of the musical impulse, does not derive from natural sound. Indeed it is its *otherness* which provides its power. Children are absorbed by and can be wrapped up in melody as it activates their right brain. Art educators speak of the attentiveness, energizing and calming effect of being absorbed by drawing as the right brain is brought into play. The right-brain mode is a source of pleasure which is hardly understood at all by neuropsychologists but which is a fundamental and universal experience. There is much evidence to show that this source of pleasure is not merely hedonistic but is a source of therapy and healing. The ability of the right brain to grasp the overall – to keep, as it were, the long distance in view – appears to contribute fundamentally to our ability to match the progress of our invented melodies in their wanderings against fixed points. It is this tying to fixed points that begins to endow such meanderings with purpose. The two fixed points are in a single pivotal pitch and in a single pivotal pulse. Although in young children's melodic improvisation (as indeed in many adults' tuneless hums and whistles) the fixed points can easily be lost, the success of such activities and, more importantly, the *feeling of success* will depend very much on whether these two fixed points of pitch and pulse have been firmly held or not.

Children invent melodies at an early age (the age of 18 months is suggested by psychologists) and a good deal of work has been done on this area (Moog, 1976; Gardner et al., 1982). Song "babbling" has interested psychologists for many years, and the beginning of musical experience and, more importantly, musical enculturation is traced back to this inherently pleasurable activity. What is most obvious to most parents is that children indulge in this kind of activity when they are happy and feeling good about themselves. We don't know which is the cause and which the effect. Not only do you invent melodies when you feel good but melody invention can make you feel good. This behaviour is observable in adult life and stays with us from our earliest days. Rodgers and Hammerstein's "Whistle a Happy Tune" has more than a grain of truth in it.

Working with individuals in a school environment

In the infant or nursery classroom, one-to-one attention is at a premium. Although such time is available it is most likely to be used in establishing essential pre-reading, reading, writing, number and essential motor skills. A few minutes spent on exploration of sound will, however, provide a child with many pathways for individual investigation. A simple activity uses a few – perhaps three – chime-bars and explores how many different patterns can be made by playing them in a different order. If the child is diffident the adult can initiate the game by playing a pattern and asking the child to imitate them, but it is best to encourage the child to take the initiative and to invent their own patterns. The adult can encourage the use of structural devices by asking, "Can you make that pattern backwards – upside down – slower – quicker – quieter – louder?" Similarly the activity can be extended by asking, "Can you add in another pitch?" and letting the child select another chime-bar, using trial and error by playing it to guide their choice. The child's power of analysis can be extended by asking, "How many notes did you play?" and "How many pitches did we use?" The child's psychomotor control can be developed through questions such as, "Can you play your pattern with this steady beat 1 – 2 – 3 – 4?"

Although the sound is being processed through the right brain, the mental activity encouraged is a mixture of left-brain logical analysis ("How many notes did you play?"), right-brain gestalt recognition ("Can you play the pattern upside down?") and psychomotor control ("Can you play your pattern with a steady beat?"). The activity also requires a physical skill of control within time. This kind of alternating between various modes of thinking and doing is the foundation of interconnectedness of thought which allows us to bring the whole brain into play.

The extension of this activity places the affective stimulus at the centre and draws on all the above skills in focusing on expressing something experienced. A child may draw patterns for their own sake, but most will wish to encapsulate something of their experience of the world by drawing. The same impulse is present in composing music: we need to express something, whether a mood, a feeling or something more concrete. Most young children choose the more concrete things. It would be more unusual for a child to paint a picture about "being happy", although this might well be the motivation. Left to their own devices children will voluntarily invent music for things which interest them at the moment. The teacher can use this impulse in them by suggesting focuses and showing that the children will gain approval by inventing something in this area. The focus will best arise from the topic currently engaging the class's interest. At a sharing time (when children show examples of their work or things of interest and discuss them with all the others) or other "carpet activity" time (when the children gather together on a mat or carpet sitting in a group in front of the teacher), children can be asked to improvise their songs with such encouragement as, "Jenny, I remember you singing a lovely song to me about going to the supermarket with Daddy the other day. Can you sing me another one now?" This will help children to become more aware of the significance of their spontaneous act. Teachers can take this a stage further, first by tape recording such songs for the children to hear them back. This provides the child with vitally needed objectivity about their own skills and personality but will need very positive handling by the teacher to avoid the severe embarrassment of unwanted exposure. Another idea is for the teacher who has some music skills to notate the song from memory or from the tape and to write it out in notation or using a computer programme. This need not be the class teacher who has initiated and collected the work but can be the teacher responsible for music in the school. The song, with the word underlay, is then mounted properly and forms part of the class's visual display. This provides important new stimulus and information about music and its recording to the class and, indeed, to parents and other teachers. The finished work should end up in the pupil's record folder or profile.

Putting sounds together

As children progress into the next stage of development, from seven onwards (Key Stage 2 in English, Welsh and Northern Irish terminology), we need to encourage a growing ability to put sounds together to make simple structures – very much in the way in which children use construction toys. Melody improvisation at the earlier key stage will already have formed a firm foundation for this work. It is normally best if limited pitches are suggested by the teacher, allowing the physical structure of the given instruments to help with melody forming. Children can also be encouraged to experiment by sorting and sequencing sounds, using pulse, tone colour and effects. Limited pitches support children in the way that bits of modular construction toys are carefully shaped to assist invention. Providing a whole chromatic instrument would be the equivalent of providing wood, nails and a hammer and waiting for a result. There will be a few children who find the openness of such a challenge stimulating, and an awareness of such special need will form part of the teacher's overall strategy.

Emphasizing structure

As children advance through Key Stage 2 and approach puberty the teacher should continue to accentuate a similar pattern of varied and contrasting composing experiments, particularly emphasizing structure. Structure can be understood both in the way that melodic ideas can conform to and derive from scalic shapes such as pentatonic, major, minor and modal, and in the overall approach to structure in thinking of the whole and the sum of the parts. At this age some children will also begin to use and formulate chordal structures, making their first experiments in harmonic flow, and structures such as ternary form and chorus and verse.

Developing the imagination

As the child becomes more confident in working with sounds and builds up a good technical "vocabulary" in their long-term memory, so it becomes more necessary to encourage and develop imagination. Imaginative play can be encouraged in more free-ranging "soundscape" experiments where the emerging individuality of the child is strengthened and encouraged. These are particularly useful as a basis for group improvisation at the top of Key Stage 2 and the bottom of Key Stage 3, since the technical core required can be fairly general, not necessarily demanding conformity to scale, key or metrical structure.

Songs, stories, journeys and maps

In the history of Western European music there are few if any examples of great music composed by pre-adolescents, but this period is central to the development of enculturation and the establishing of long-term memory patterns and predispositions and techniques. During this period teachers should expect leaps of understanding to be taken in both directions interspersed with plateaus. There does seem to be a need for pre-pubertal children to revisit some learning processes; it is almost as if they have gone too far and need to recoil before jumping off into adolescence. It may well be that the change of school which takes place for very many children at this age acts as a catalyst, and certainly my personal experience in the state education system (with transfer at the age of 11) has led me to these conclusions. Perhaps they are less apparent in middle schools and independent preparatory schools.

In any case learning is a messy business. Despite theoretical structures such as the Swanwick–Tillman proposition of a spiral of musical development, children constantly surprise us by their sudden insights and regressions. The capacity of individual children of eight to 14 to produce individual compositions is enormous, particularly those who have instrumental lessons. Instrumental teachers can help establish the notion of improvising by asking their pupils to invent exercises and expressive pieces within their own capabilities as players, but only recently have such teachers begun to take this side of their work seriously – although Fanny Waterman, for instance, used the technique with her pupils in the 1960s and 1970s. Her well-known piano tutors contain many examples of young students' compositions. Pupils who have no instrumental facility at all are seriously disadvantaged as potential composers.

The class teacher can help to bridge the gap between instrumental tuition and curriculum music education by giving those children who have the privilege of instrumental tuition the responsibility to lead composing groups or to produce work such as songs for the whole class to sing. Improvisation can be assisted greatly if the pupil has some instrumental skill. More often than not such children also play the recorder and can tackle pitched percussion easily. Giving such children an organizing and motivating responsibility in class composing may well offer them a chance to use their skills to shine among their peers as an alternative to the more traditional forms of sporting prowess.

Songs and stories really come into their own at this large stage of development, and increasingly it will be the child's own imagination that will fire the creation of new music. Once it becomes a normal activity in the classroom for someone or for a group to express themselves in musical creation, much will happen that is spontaneous, just as we find with story, poetry writing, painting and constructing.

Composing tasks which flow directly from some focus or topic play an important part of the exploration around a theme, which is still a standard part of school practice despite the subject orientation of the National Curriculum. Cross-curricular links can very well be strengthened by the setting of a composing task for a group or individual children. The interrelationship between history, geography, science and maths and music are all fairly easy to explore. Making a song about a historical event is very much within the tradition of ballads, the story of a river's birth and growth is a popular musical structure, the harmonic series and the intervals and scales deriving from it provide the equivalent of musical Lego from which constructions can be made, and the division of a beat into fractions can be the motivating force for a percussion improvisation.

Journeys and stories are very similarly constructed, although a journey emphasizes the element of time and is sequential in the way that music behaves. The act of walking is considered by some to be a fundamental musical principle, wonderfully described by Bruce Chatwin in *The Songlines*.

In any journey there are constants and surprises. The constant is our movement, whether walking, riding or driving. We move from place to place and when we arrive somewhere we find something new. Some journeys may revisit the same places at times, but the chorus and verse structure of a journey provides a great balance between repetition and new discovery. Journeys make very good musical construction kits, and the imaginative teacher will seize on opportunities to make real journeys their parallel in musical inventions. The normal journey to school in the morning, the school camp trip, a visit to the zoo, a delivery lorry on its rounds, a pony ride in the country and a tube train ride all provide potential musical structures. Sometimes the locations visited can be conveyed in soundscapes; sometimes known material may be used, such as song melodies already learnt in class and rediscovered on instruments.

Using story-board sequences can be helpful in establishing structural balance and formal relationships. Story-boards are well-tried teaching devices in story-writing and tend to encourage a rather basic response from the student. Perhaps this is why they are commonly used in the

That man is a migratory species is, in my opinion, borne out by an experiment made at the Tavistock Clinic in London and described by Dr John Bowlby in his *Attachment and Loss*.

Every normal baby will scream if left alone; and the best way of silencing these screams is for the mother to take it in her arms and rock or "walk" it back to contentment. Bowlby rigged up a machine which imitated, exactly, the pace and action of a mother's walk; and found that, providing the baby was healthy, warm and well-fed, it stopped crying at once. "The ideal movement", he wrote, "is a vertical one with a traverse of three inches." Rocking at slow speeds, such as thirty cycles a minute, had no effect: but once you raised the pace to fifty and above, every baby ceased to cry and almost stayed quiet.

Apes have flat feet, we have sprung arches. According to Professor Napier, the human gait is a long, lilting stride – 1 ... 2, ... 1 ... 2 – with a fourfold rhythm built into the action of the feet as they come in contact with the ground – 1, 2, 3, 4 ... 1, 2, 3, 4 ...: heel strike; weight along the outside of the foot; weight transferred to the ball of the foot; push-off with the big toe.

The question occurs to me – and quite seriously – how many shoe soles, how many ox-hide soles, how many sandals Alighieri wore out in the course of his poetic work, wandering about on the goat paths of Italy.

The *Inferno* and especially the *Purgatorio* glorify the human gait, the measure and rhythm of walking, the foot and its shape. The step, linked to the breathing and saturated with thought: this Dante understands as the beginning of prosody.

Osip Mandelstam, Conversations about Dante, quoted in Chatwin (1987).

Regardless of the words, it seems the melodic contour of the song described the nature of the land over which the song passes. So, if the Lizard Man were dragging his heels across the salt-pans of Lake Eyre, you would expect a succession of long flats, like Chopin's Funeral March. If he were skipping up and down the MacDonnell escarpments, you'd have a series of arpeggios and glissandos, like Liszt's "Hungarian Rhapsodies".

Certain phrases, certain combinations of musical notes, are thought to describe the action of the Ancestor's *feet.* One phrase would say, "Salt-pan"; another "Creek-bed", "Spinifex", "Sand-hill", "Mulga-scrub", "Rock-face bed", and so forth. An expert song-man, by listening to their order of succession, would count how many times his hero crossed a river or scaled a ridge – and be able to calculate where, and how far along, a Songline he was.

"He'd be able", said Arkady, "to hear a few bars, and say 'This is Middle Bore' or 'That is Oodnadatta' – where the Ancestor did X or Y or Z."

"So a musical phrase", I said, "is a map reference?"

"Music", said Arkady, "is a memory bank for finding one's way about the world."

"I shall need some time to digest that."

"You've got all night", he smiled. "With the snakes!"

Chatwin (1987).

first steps of second-language teaching. The response of the student is more usually left-brain centred and proposes factual descriptions of the pictures given. Story-boarding in music has the potential of forcing a metaphorical relationship from the outset between picture and music. What must be guarded against is the natural impulse to take a left-brain approach and to describe as accurately as possible any real sounds conveyed. In a typical example, a sequence of seven pictures show 1) a house in a street in early evening with a light snow fall; 2) a dog looking lost in heavier falling snow; 3) the house in heavy snow fall; 4) the dog looking in at a party through a window; 5) a house in a blizzard; 6) the dog in a blizzard; 7) the dog at the door of his house being welcomed by his master. In this example it would be the sound of the wind, the whining of the dog and the song everyone imagines is being played at the party. By placing a ban on these from the start – no direct imitation of anything – a more balanced approach between right and left brain can be encouraged.

Before commissioning this piece of work the teacher should explore with the class or group the story-board's structure. The class should decide what elements are common and where there are special features. An important issue in this example is the difference in function between foreground and background – in music, solo and accompaniment. The next step is for the teacher to ask the children what feelings each picture gives and to question how such feelings could be conveyed in music through melody, rhythm, tone colour, texture and harmony. The rest should be up to the group, although they sometimes need help in choosing a soloist and find the decision difficult socially.

Maps provide a more complex analogy. Bruce Chatwin, again from *The Songlines*, describes the practice of linking maps and musical experience in detail as it is found in the lives of native Australians. Another process of musical mapping is described by Simon Waters, in *Living Without Boundaries*:

"In addition to the widely understood cartographical sense of making a representation of a geographical surface, indicating its features, there is an equally significant (for the arts) metaphorical sense of the term from mathematics, this referring to the association of each element of one system or set (of objects, processes, values) with that from another system or set. One might, for example, map a series of numbers which refer to the dimensions and proportions of a building onto a series of musical note values, or use them to determine the proportions of a musical structure.

Converting some shape or other, the school building for instance, into a set of numbers, and then mapping those onto a musical matrix can provide challenging aesthetic problems. The musical matrix in question needs also to be converted into a set of numbers, and this can be done simply by giving each pitch a value and the basic rhythmic segment a value (let's say, for argument, the sixteenth). It's the sort of job best performed with the aid of a step-time computer sequencer which can perform the, very likely, weird musical results. In Chatwin's Australian example the melodic contour is analogous to the actual contours of the countryside rather in the way that some of the Welsh countryside contours have always seemed to me to emerge from the contour of "Ar Hyd y Nos". Those who know the silhouette of Pen-y-Fan in the Brecon

Beacons may understand what I am saying. Melodic contours could well be created for well-known journeys to school or within the environment.

Another form of mapping derives from accurate and analytical listening and will be based on a chosen pre-recorded musical example. One that I like to use is "Max's Sea Journey" from Oliver Knussen's opera *Where the Wild Things Are*, based on Maurice Sendak's book of the same name. The description of a lesson, or lessons, in Example 3 in the previous chapter shows how this listening and notating activity is interlocked and integral to the composing activity.

At the beginning of Key Stage 3 (11 to 14 years) play must be balanced by advancing technical learning. At this stage of schooling it is most vital to stimulate and motivate children towards personal expression, and as the child approaches adolescence it becomes more important to assist the ability to express musical meaning in adult terms. Although an awareness of experimental and avant-garde music should be encouraged, music which the majority of pre-adolescent and adolescent children will consider to be more "grown up", such as blues and other folk and jazz-derived forms, will be strongly attractive. There should be a focus on the music of today's society, not defined exclusively as the music of today's youth culture, which is too particular and largely ephemeral, but emphasizing the foundations of music that is popular generally.

Making music your own

Composing techniques should become so well absorbed by the end of Key Stage 3 that the young person begins to combine and use them in an integrated and unconscious way, making their own new combinations of sounds and building up a peculiarly personal choice of chords, melodic phrases, rhythmic quirks and, sometimes, eventually their own original systems. There is plenty of evidence that, in early adolescence, some young people can produce outstanding compositions. Mendelssohn's music to Shakespeare's *A Midsummer Night's Dream* falls into this category, as perhaps do Britten's "Quatre Chansons Françaises" (written in 1928), and while these are exceptional examples they nonetheless give us ultimate yardsticks of achievement. Obligatory composition in public examinations at 16 and 18 is showing increasingly the potential of young people to be original thinkers.

Balancing theory and practice

I am in no doubt about the responsibility of music specialists in the secondary school to build up skills in the manipulation of traditional Western notation, which is rapidly becoming used in societies worldwide. It would be a nonsense to see the development of the interest in World Music as a one-way process, East to West so to speak, and it is obvious that there is an enormously expanding interest in Western music in the East, together with a strong ability to absorb and practise our culture and its methods of notation. It is important that our own society is not left standing, as it were, and unable to use its own traditional skills. Balancing the curriculum design sensitively between theory and practice has been very difficult but it should always be at the forefront of our thinking.

During Key Stage 3 it is important to build up the conceptual understanding of traditional structures, such as scales, keys and modes, for instance, and to cultivate notational skills in reading and writing. A firm foundation built at this stage will allow the details of technical expression to be dealt with during Key Stage 4, where, at the moment, it is necessary to build up rather more basic concepts and techniques. If teachers could approach their work in Key Stage 4 with more confidence that ground work had been done, there would be less problem in moving on into "A"-Level (Highers in Scotland) for those students who choose to do so, and this would also make "AS"-Level (Supplementary) music exams a more attractive and viable alternative for those students whose main interest lies in other disciplines but who do not wish to lose sight of music. As a general rule, teachers underestimate children, and the experience of GCSE has clearly demonstrated that, if you trust to the innate abilities of children and provide them with the right stimulus and working environment, they are capable of far more than many of us ever dreamed.

Composing beyond the age of 14

In considering starting-points for pieces of composing at the more advanced stage, the tasks can be varied and more intellectually demanding than before. For the rest of the period in education the need to exercise skills and to use techniques is very intense and there must be plenty of chance for students to engage in imitative and formal exercises alongside the more open and challenging projects. Pastiche or imitative writing can be of great use at this stage, especially if the range of styles is open enough and the students have a large and secure enough memory bank of such styles. Teachers should always start from where the students are and must establish which of those styles are well known and popular. Current hit-parade material may well produce extra-musical problems, as previously explained, but other shared vernaculars such as musical comedy or "musicals" can be fruitful sources for pastiche. Closed projects such as "Write a song about … It must have a middle eight in a related key and should express …" can be easily deconstructed from a given model. Harmony charts taken from an unspecified but tried and tested classic rock number (preferably one not known well by the students) can present a closed experiment in composing together with a list of nouns or adjectives extracted from lyrics. The project is to invent a song which uses the chord sequence and which will contain all the words in the lyrics; neither harmonic sequence nor words are given in order but an overall key is set.

Composing at advanced levels

Although students may enter advanced examination or degree courses with a great deal of experience as performers, despite the changing nature of our curriculum the majority of students will still deny their own skills in composing. Teachers at this level have to be prepared to revisit first principles of composing yet again, as I have already suggested for entry into Key Stage 3, and although a great deal of child-like work will need to take place, the skilled teacher can commission this in a way in which the students' sense of identity is enhanced. Students in further and higher education are most commonly strongly inhibited about themselves as beginners in a new education process. Learning how to begin again and benefit from it is perhaps one of the greatest survival skills in education.

All of the principles stated above apply equally well to further and higher education. Group work is important and can be very successful at this stage of development, since many of the problems of social interaction inherent in younger adolescents will have disappeared. This is not to suggest that cooperative working practices do not have to be openly discussed. The problems of both dominance and reticence are very obvious at this age-level, but the maturity of the group should make it far easier for the teacher not only to address these matters, but to use them to the student's advantage.

In planning individual assignments the practice of commissioning should be the main principle. Commissioning is what real composers are used to. Commissions should be practical, reflecting the real world of work, and teachers need to think this through and note changing practices. The commission for a commercial jingle will be very different in kind from the commission for a string quartet. Style should be an essential ingredient of any commission, whether free or determined, and students need to learn to turn their hand to any piece of stylistic writing required while still preserving their own identity. Commissions for television, film and radio usually give broad stylistic guidelines and rarely leave things completely open. Commissions for various ensembles will be moderated by proposed venue of performance and the special needs of the performers. Work written for the ICA will differ from that written for the regional music club circuit. Everything that a student writes needs to be heard, and students should be dissuaded from creating huge castles in the air by writing for impossible forces or for virtuosi performers who are not at hand. Rather, students should learn to write for other students, noting their strengths and weaknesses and building on these. The inclusion of student works in major concert events is a great motivator.

The need for a balance between open and closed experiments and for a good deal of copying or pastiche work to continue is strong. Pastiche allows students to build up a bank of available techniques and to put them into practice without sacrificing too much of their own individuality. As a practice it is tried and tested, but too often in the past it has been allowed to dominate the teaching of composing, and most particularly it became associated with the practice of students working in silence away from the sound source. Action research has proved time and again that, when students are able to resort to keyboards or other sound sources, and therefore to engage their ear as well as their memory as arbiter, the standard of work improves greatly. The ability to reproduce this in a silent examination room is a false skill which is unnecessary and never very useful in real life. Encouraging the application of logical techniques using guess work and trialling, which is what using keyboards allows, maximizes both left- and right-brain patterns.

Resumé

- The first principle is that of forming aural concepts in the head – sometimes called internalization – which must be particularly carefully encouraged by good teaching strategies. Using right-brain techniques to imagine music in the head first, not in detail, but in large overall shapes, is an important technique to be established early in young composers.

- Composition pupils respond very quickly to the teacher's willingness to give what they have done serious thought and attention. Teachers need to be most careful to approach any negatives through positive strategies, especially in the early stages.

- A movement backwards and forwards between right- and left-brain processes, while always giving the advantage to the right brain through focused attention on sound, intuitive thought and holistic planning of many kinds, provides the best model for the composition teacher. The final arbiter of success is in the right brain's intuition and affective response, since this was also the initiator, and the process of assessment mirrors this.

- Composition proceeds through constant interaction between the two opposed brain hemispheres, where the left brain provides us with ability to produce detail and to record it with accuracy, and the right brain monitors and considers the effect of the detail upon the whole. The more composing becomes a remote and specialized task, the more it is inclined to become left-brain oriented, reliant on notation or, for some now, computer-stored information.

- A predominantly right-brained vernacular approach based on sound and musical memory should be encouraged by teachers, since it provides the most potent foundation for all future skills. Although pupils may well be engaged in arranging and producing parodies or pastiches, as they may be in literature studies or art, their own individual creative work can only stem from the musical language with which they feel comfortable.

- The technical disciplines, experienced through sound, cannot be side-stepped, and teachers must plan input of technical know-how and experience throughout a child's school life.

- The single line of melody is the musical basis of all composition and this can be traced through clear evidence in all cultures. Children naturally improvise song and, when left, or encouraged, to conserve and record their music, will record only the pitch and general presentation of shape and structure. Precise rhythm is left to the memory or word rhythms. Accurate recording of pitch can always be checked against an instrument, and is therefore mostly right brain in operation, but that for rhythm depends on an abstract conceptual process which draws heavily upon left-brain procedures.

- The basic compositional structural unit is song. Songs and stories are related generically. Early sound experiments stem from a process of describing and naming. Concrete musical thinking produces one-to-one matching of stimulus and response. Many first experiments in sound by children draw upon ready-made symbolism. Children's earliest sound explorations will be limited by the shape and construction of the sound resources used.

- Adults notice, encourage and even preserve early mark-making of children far more than they do sound-pattern-making. Children invent melodies at an early age. Working with individuals, adults can help children conserve their work by encouraging repetition, by use of tape recordings or in notation.

- Melody improvisation at the earlier key stage will already have formed a firm foundation for making larger musical structures at Key Stage 2.

Imaginative play can be encouraged in more free-ranging "soundscape" experiments. The class teacher can help to bridge the gap between instrumental tuition and curriculum music education by giving those children who have the privilege of instrumental tuition the responsibility to lead composing groups or to produce work such as songs for the whole class to sing.

- Cross-curricular links can very well be strengthened by the setting of a composing task for a group or individual children. Journeys make very good musical construction kits, and the imaginative teacher will seize on opportunities to make real journeys their parallel in musical inventions. Using story-board sequences can be helpful in establishing structural balance and formal relationships.

- Composing techniques should become so well absorbed by the end of Key Stage 3 that the young person begins to combine and use them in an integrated and unconscious way.

- It is the responsibility of music specialists in the secondary school to build up skills in the manipulation of traditional Western notation as well as the conceptual understanding of traditional structures such as scales, keys and modes.

- Pastiche or imitative writing can be of great use beyond Key Stage 3, especially if the range of styles is open enough and the students have a large and secure enough memory bank of such styles. Teachers should always start from where the students are and must establish which of those styles are well known and popular.

- In planning individual assignments the practice of commissioning should be the main principle. Commissions should be practical, reflecting the real world of work. The need for a balance between open and closed experiments and for a good deal of copying or pastiche work to continue is strong.

Teaching implications

Organizing learning: individual – group – individual

It will always be useful to bear in mind that we start the composing work of young children as individuals, and, as they pass up through the system, they experience various working practices in pairs, threes and larger groups, gaining through the discussion and stimulus, but also being subjected to the organizational imperative imposed by the local conditions of their school's provision. In the secondary phase pupils reach that sensitive age of adolescence when their individualism and sense of identity matter to them perhaps more than anything else, and teachers should be very aware of the need to encourage individual work and enterprise; this may not mean waiting until examination specialization. It is important that all teachers carry a concern for individual work throughout all age-levels, but it is of particular importance in the secondary stage where pressures of time and resources militate against it. There is no method that will automatically ensure caring for individual development. With the principle firmly at heart, the successful teacher will find ways of encouraging individual enterprise through projects, homework, performances and other motivation and stimulus.

Exploration of materials

The initial stages of exploration of materials are vested in experiments with sound, especially those dealing with the impressiveness of tone colour and dynamic, which are encouraged above other features. These are the musical equivalence of sand and water play. First steps usually involve the teacher leading the whole group in improvisation as a "carpet activity", but the real idea of composing must be experienced by the children by involving them individually in musical problem-solving and getting them used to the idea that they can manipulate the medium for themselves. Sound spill can be a serious hazard in this activity, and children need to be taught the same disciplines in use of musical equipment that also govern the use of other essential materials. Working in nearby outdoor areas alongside sand and water play can be a great help in reducing sound spill, when the weather allows. Teachers need to be very sensitive to the results of a child either abusing their privilege in playing musical sounds, or merely being carried away with the sensuous properties of the sound, oblivious to its effect on others. The stress level on both teacher and pupils must be a particular consideration, and such exploratory work can only take place when conditions are right.

Music corner activities

A space in the infant and junior classroom needs to be set aside for music work by individuals and pairs. Music corners should not be seen as housing areas for all the music equipment but should be reserved for specific tasks set up by the teacher. Such tasks will normally follow on from class-initiated work, and the children should be used to finding at the music corner appropriate instruments and instructions. These spaces can also house listening facilities for individuals, both players and cassettes, clearly labelled, and, for older children, some listening tasks.

Music corner activities need to be very supportive and clearly defined – as small an "open end" as possible – and the element of exploration of sound, in as much as it can be freely encouraged in a busy infant classroom, should be emphasized only within well-defined limits. Tasks may include performing an ostinato learnt in the lesson, inventing a melody using a structure that has been explored, or making an imaginative sound picture extension of work in the class.

Copying as a methodolgy

Copying is one of the most powerful forms of learning. It is the way in which all children learn to speak and to perform most vital functions. The last few decades have rather dismissed the notion of copying directly out of hand as being unindividualist and slavish in conception. History, however, provides us with many examples of the need to learn through copying and of its power as a learning experience. In the past, European student painters have been employed in the studios of established painters, working on their large canvases as apprentices and submitting their own personal expression to the task in hand. Although painters in the twentieth century appear largely to have dismissed this method of apprenticeship, early works of many of them show how important the following of stylistic models has been to them. It has been continuing practice in ceramics and sculpture for students to work alongside the established artist; Moore, Hepworth and Leach are obvious examples. Mozart's early works stay very close to fashionable models and Wagner spent many hours of his youth copying out and arranging Beethoven's music. Left to themselves, our young people from Key Stage 2 onwards can also feel safest in making their first steps in creative music-making by copying. The so-called cover versions of current or past hit numbers are the staple diet of emergent rock bands. Copying may be in total or only in part, conscious or unconscious. Teachers should never be worried by what might appear, to their adult ears, a lack of originality or novelty. To the young composer experiencing things for the first time, much of the unconscious and even the conscious copying is imbued with a freshness of experience that makes it feel totally theirs.

As children begin to remember and to copy musical sequences, these sequences of sound begin to take on meaning for them through being drawn into the long-term memory. Once they are firmly established and available for deconstruction and reconstruction, children begin to use such memories in making their own first constructions in order to help them find out how they think and feel about the world, and there is a direct parallel here with speaking, reading and creative writing.

Common musical language

The more patterns, sequences and phrases are stored in the brain the more they begin to link into and move towards that musical expression which is usual and accepted in the child's environment. Swanwick and Tillman (1986) use the term "vernacular" to mean music which is the common factor in any child's environment. For most children this will mean not just "pop" music, which is only one stylistic manifestation of the underlying vernacular that is tonal, metrical and simple harmonic music, but any music which conforms to these structures. This applies as much to nursery rhymes as it does to rap music or songs from the shows, and what they know will depend upon what they hear and have heard at home and in their community. For a significant minority the vernacular may be tonal and metrical but will conform to other cultural models, perhaps of Asian or African origin. Whatever their vernacular is, as they grow, children will increasingly wish to make their musical structures conform to these models.

Open and closed composing activities

Care must always be taken to balance composing activities between those which could be seen as "closed" activities, intended to give practice in technique and exercise in the logics of music, and those which could be called "open" activities, where the imagination and macro-thinking powers of children are most challenged. Closed activities emphasize left-brain technical learning and provide a very limited and supportive set of circumstances, whereas the open activities provide imaginative stimulus for the right brain in circumstances designed also to maximize the left-brain technical experience gained. The sequence of activities provided by the sensitive teacher should swing backwards and forwards between these two modes. This should be viewed as giving preference sometimes to the left brain, sometimes to the right, but always emphasizing the need for both to integrate.

Stravinsky – "in art as in everything else you can build only upon a firm resisting foundation ... So my liberty consists in moving inside the narrow bounds which I set for myself for each thing I undertake."

Ferguson (1973).

Organizing group work

Of late the trend in upper primary and secondary age classes has been to divide up the class into small groups and for these groups to work together for the majority of the time. Although this manner of working has a central place in the composing curriculum, there are several problems with this method of which all teachers need to be aware, and it is important to plan carefully for such modes of working. The following procedures should be observed.

Setting the task

It is important to consider the vital role played by input and modelling at the start of any composing lesson sequence. Too often teachers ignore this, with the consequence that groups can be set tasks without clear models and goals given to them by the teacher, and they can then be easily allowed far more time than is needed to fulfil the task set. The answer to this problem is first to be found in a clearly defined task, initial idea or stimulus. This requires thought, preparation and the building up by the teacher of tried materials over a period of time. It should also take its place in a rational plan of the overall composing curriculum.

Modelling the task

The teacher must be aware of the need for clear demonstration first, and it is often better to work with the whole class on some sort of model improvisation with the teacher as the *animateur* or group leader. This way teachers pass on to the students clear procedural guidance and technical know-how which otherwise can be neglected. There is a danger, of course, of the model being too dominant, but in the first stages it is far better for this to happen than for disorganized work to depress both teacher and the students. An antidote to unwanted dominance lies in the teacher's use of language, for example, "In this situation you might do this or you may choose to do that. If this, then ..."

Forming groups

Teachers need to decide on the method of selection of groups and also the optimum size. Normally a group should have no more than six at Key Stage 3, but research has also shown clearly that pairing is one of the most successful methods of working for results over short time-blocks. The choice of groups may be at random, may maximize instrumental skills by allotting such students to each group, or may depend on friendship grouping or proceed by opposites, for example, low skilled paired with high skilled. Teachers may wish to consider streaming but will need to review the overall tasks with care to make certain that differentiation is apparent. We must never forget that the eventual outcome must be individual work, and this must be planned for over the whole of Key Stages 3 and 4.

Cooperative working skills

Cooperative working is a skill which is important, and teachers need to promote this in their curriculum. It is not necessarily something that just happens, and there is much evidence that teachers need positively to teach these skills by discussing problems with both the group in question and the whole class. The problems of overdominance are common, as are those of reticence, and it has been shown that, with the teacher acting as catalyst, such problems can often best be addressed by the children themselves. Social education of this kind is an important part of all teachers' work, and the problem-solving nature of composition gives it a high profile in today's core skills.

The teacher's role

Having introduced and modelled working techniques in an open-ended way, the teacher has a threefold task: a) observing, b) recording, c) intervening.

Plenary sessions

Action research into music education practice by teachers over several years has shown that on return to the plenary session many groups "improvise" a result which bears little relationship to what they have spent all their time on. An instant result is improvised for the sake of the exercise. This is often the product of frustration from the children when tasks are too open-ended, too easy/difficult, or too remote in their achievable result from any acceptable real-world model.

Review

The key to the successful plenary session lies with teachers and the comments made by them as soon as the music stops. This is the most sensitive time and is the point where so many teachers fail the children. Positive attitudes are vital since it is the teacher's job to make people feel as good about themselves as they can when it is justified. However, just to accept work as good because something active has happened is equally unacceptable. Teachers must try to have an acceptable standard clear in their head and should not hesitate to criticize when this is not reached, particularly when they know that it is within the capability of their students to reach it. By reserving this for the rare and just occasions when it is applicable the disapproval will be most effective. The most important element in feedback is what the children themselves say, and it is in this review work that real learning can be reinforced through the teacher encouraging helpful critiques from other children.

Finally the teacher should draw together the threads of the topic relating back to the learning core for which he or she has planned and making it obvious to each pupil how far they have progressed and what they have learnt. Making learning manifest is an important part of the proceedings, since quite often children will not realize what it is they have been learning from the activity in which they have been engaged. Making this manifest has a very particular function in fixing the learning.

Use of space

If teachers do not have separate work spaces for group work, then the amount of whole-group work with them as *animateur* – or a student in that place – should increase proportionally. It really is not good to have several groups all playing against each other at the same time, even though many students have the ability to "switch off" all the surrounding sound. If teachers are forced into this kind of activity through geographical circumstances then they must evolve very strict disciplines in instrument use. Many teachers encourage too much active experiment and not enough internalized thinking and imagining sound, especially as the students move up through the school years. In these circumstances it is very worth while making best use of space by exploring the notion of the mixed economy music curriculum which maximizes equipment and can make the best use of limited space. In even more cramped conditions there comes a time when the room determines the curriculum, and then this is a job for senior management teams and governors on the teacher's advice.

Assessment

Assessment records should be kept from the first weeks in school and should carry a profile of each child. As the National Curriculum practice grows there should be increasing records arising from the primary school. It is important to feed in records from visiting instrumental teachers and also to use these records diagnostically. Music education can be helpful in spotting potential in students not otherwise apparent in other areas and can be vital in building their self-esteem. It can also be very specific in diagnosing problems and is just as useful a marker as the more traditional language or number skills, since music utilizes all the learning areas, affective, cognitive and kinaesthetic, and demands a unique coordination of all three.

One of the key contributors to continuous assessment must be the student herself or himself. Wherever possible there should be feedback from the student to the teacher as well as in the more normal teacher to student direction. This can be effected through journals, or through formal work records, which can be done regularly or can be instituted occasionally. The school's own chosen method of records of achievement may well help to determine the appropriate system. The encouragement of ownership and the pride in one's own achievement which is attendant upon this cannot be underestimated, and this will never fully take place unless children feel themselves to be part of the process of determination of their futures. Composing in the music education curriculum has the most potential to promote such a feeling and for that reason alone can be well justified. Occasional formal evaluations by the students of the teacher's own practice can be very illuminating, and it often surprises teachers that the vast majority of students take this responsibility very seriously.

Example 1: Making a soundscape with young children

Lesson focus: Composing – form, tone colour
Resources: Voices, found sounds and/or instruments

In a carpet activity, the children are shown a sequence of pictures prepared by the teacher. The children look at the sequence of pictures, which in this case tell the story of Flood, and they discuss it with their teacher. The key questions are:

● how does this picture make you feel?
● how might we make musical sounds with our voices which sound the way that feels?

The discussion that inevitably follows compares appropriate sounds with the answers the children have given. The first approach is to ask the children to think about, discuss and make sounds for each of the pictures using only their voices. This allows for and encourages exploration of voice pitch and tone quality and keeps the thinking about sound at the most conceptual level possible. For example, the last picture is a very peaceful one with a rainbow in a clear sky. Making peaceful sounds with the voice is something we all understand and can try to do. A long held hummed note, joined to the next by a very quick breath and held as steadily as possible, is the key musical image. A sensitive teacher will enhance the musical effect by providing a strong tonal centre for the children to focus upon with her own voice. She can also help the children to experience the sound getting louder or fading away.

Single-note humming engages the child in the most intimate, intuitive and least concrete musical experience and can engender a strong feeling of satisfaction after completion. It is strong right-brain material and provides everyone with a feeling of involvement. Indeed it can sometimes result in a clearly changed state of consciousness which can last for some time after the event. Such emptying the mind of concrete thought and replacing it with contact with something other than concrete thought is a fundamental artistic experience. Not all the children will be able to respond to the pitch-centre focus, and the resultant sound can be a humming conglomerate of sounds which can be very satisfying in its own right.

The other pictures will engender many other sounds of an onomatopoeic version. Again, what the teacher can add to the children's individual suggestions and ideas is sequencing and overall control. The wave sounds, for instance, can start quietly and rise up in volume. A decision to repeat a pattern of wave sounds, for example, "Splosh, crash, break, scrunch", and to make a rise in the pitch and volume of the voice up to "break" and then slipping down again, can be made by the teacher through discussion with the children. The overall structure, sequence and coordination of this whole collection of sounds then needs to be organized. The children can then be asked to find ways in sound of linking the last picture with the first so that the composition has a beginning which relates to its ending.

Once everyone has enjoyed making and redefining this improvisation until it becomes a fixed piece of composing, the teacher suggests that the children should make their own picture of their music. A wall frieze is created with whatever additions the children suggest, remembering that such additions must have their own sound counterpart. An extension will be to add instrumental and found sounds to the vocal sounds we already have. When it comes to an actual performance of our piece we are able to play from our own "score", using the frieze or the photographs and appointing a child (or the teacher) to point to the section we are playing as we play it.

Although in this lesson the first stimulus was through the eye, the important focal activity has been with the ear. Most importantly, the children have been stimulated to imagine and reproduce sounds linked with intuitions and feelings. If words have been used they have been used not for their naming qualities but for their onomatopoeic or sounding qualities. All these provide a good diet for the right brain.

The sequencing and packaging of sounds into discrete structures, repeated sections and sections that relate all begin to engage the left brain in musical decision-making, and sensori-motor control is engaged as soon as we make sounds with our voices. If we add instruments then this area is enhanced. The frieze the class makes and can then play from is the movement back to the eye, once the sound patterns are committed to memory and the associated movements are rehearsed. A holistic musical experience has been given fusing together complementary brain functions.

Example 2: Starting with a class approach and commissioning individual tasks at the end of Key Stage 1 or the beginning of Key Stage 2

Lesson focus: Composing for Divali
Resources: Five chime-bars, drum

The class is sitting as for story time on the carpet, with the teacher on a chair. The children have learnt the story of Divali and have discussed the feelings of Rama and Sita on arrival back at the city of their banishment. They talk with their teacher about the sight of the twinkling lights in the streets as they emerge from the forest on their elephant. Having learnt the Divali Song and explored the pitch and rhythm patterns (see Appendix) they are asked by the teacher, "How do you think the elephant felt towards the end of that journey? What did the elephant feel when it saw the path with the lights leading towards home? What sort of sounds would best describe the elephant walking? Would they be fast or slow? Would they be steady beats or not?"

The teacher places a few chime-bars, say five, in front of the children and asks individuals to think about and play some patterns which will make us think of the elephant's tired feet as it walks along. "How many pitches should we use?" (Four would be logical!) "Can you make up a pattern using four different tones? Can you make it repeat?" After several children have explored this with success and can repeat it, say, three times with a good steady beat, the teacher asks, " Who can think of some words to describe that elephant's feelings?" (For example – *tired and hungry*.)

The teacher then helps the children to speak the words against a steady beat on a drum. Having done this successfully a musical structure can be set up with the children, starting with, for example, three repeats of the four-tone pattern against a steady beat on the drum, followed by three repeats of the words, finished off by three repeats of the four-tone pattern.

Individual work is then initiated by the teacher suggesting that individuals or pairs of children can use the music table at appropriate times during the week to invent their own patterns for the elephant, who may well have a name by this time! It will be very usual for some children to ask to use other instruments as well, and the teacher must gauge the appropriateness of this to the overall well-being of the class, for instance, in the case of loud cymbals. It will be necessary to make a professional judgement as to whether the children are adding to the task through creative thinking or are diverting from the task through replacing thinking with just doing.

As each individual or pair of children meets with success and has played their work to the teacher, the teacher then asks them to find some way of writing down their composition so that they can remember it. If the teacher has marked the chime-bars with Sol-fa pitches (doh, re, mi, etc.) the children may well use these names as an integral part of their music. If they have used a selection of sound sources it is quite likely that the children will try to draw pictures of these. Three tambourine-like drawings in a line could well mean "Play the tambourine three times." Written words can be equally useful if the children can use them with ease. Children should be encouraged to use drawings and colours in recording their music, and it is not necessary that the record should follow the normal logic of writing from left to right, although children who know something of reading and writing mostly do this.

Each successful piece of work should be played to the whole class if the composer/performers are willing, but it would be wrong to insist on this with some more reticent children. The composition can be stored in one of two ways. Firstly the written "score" should be mounted, titled and displayed on the wall or in books/a folder as appropriate to the normal practice. Secondly the best pieces of work should be tape recorded by the teacher to be stored in the individual's personal folder, appropriately labelled with date and details of the work done.

Example 3: An open-ended project at Key Stage 3

Lesson focus: Improvising a score for an imaginary television drama
Resources: Keyboards, recording equipment, a variety of instruments, plenty of ancillary space to the main music room

This open project for a class of 13- or 14-year-olds is to invent jointly the music for an imaginary television film. They should be given a local legend, or a well-known simple enough story, and the teacher asks the class to imagine that they have the task to turn this into a television film. The first step is to divide the story up into the necessary sections, preferably matching the number of sections with the most manageable numbers of groups. This will be determined by group size and by available working space. The project works equally well with individuals.

Once the scenes and their timing have been decided upon, work can begin on initial improvisations. During plenary sessions the students make choices and suggestions and evolve some ingredients jointly that will bind together the whole. This can be the tonal centre or centres, melodic fragments, harmonies, textures, effects and so on. Ideas need to be stimulated in the group by the teacher, who must also not feel reticent in making helpful suggestions.

Over some weeks of work the individual scenes need to be finalized and performed, capturing the best attempts on tape. Each group should be encouraged to treat the whole class as a potential orchestra and choir and to invent material which can be taught to and performed by the whole group in the plenary and recording sessions.

The ultimate crown of such a project is to make the video as well and then to edit it to the music tape. This has been done most successfully by Cape Cornwall Secondary School through a project on the Mermaid of Zennor. This project took a whole term in the classroom and a further day filming at Zennor. The final video was produced early in the next term by the groups who invented the music editing their own version.

Example 4: A cross-curricular project for upper secondary pupils

Lesson focus: The interactiveness between visual art and music
Resources: Reproductions of paintings/art works, instruments

A discussion with the pupils explains that there are interesting comparative relationships between visual work and music and conceptual areas in both art disciplines may be usefully compared. The right-brain perception of musical tonality and its varied use to underpin musical structures across all cultures makes an interesting comparison with that of perspective in two-dimensional visual work. The notion of a single vanishing point governing all the sets of design relationships within a drawing or painting is directly aligned psychologically with the notion that one chosen fixed pitch ties all other pitches into a tonal relationship with it.

The project for a group or for individuals can start from a postcard reproduction or poster or, even better, of an original art work. The analysis which must follow needs to pursue the path of metaphoric relationships and analogies and not to consider as at all important either the title or obvious subject matter of the picture. It is preferable to choose examples which are not figurative at first. The following comparisons are signposts to the type of analysis which can be of most help to a musician.

Line in visual art and melodic contour in music both present metaphors of movement in space and time, the first in two dimensions, the second in time only. The **intensity** of a piece of music in terms of both volume and timbre presents useful analogies to qualities and depths of **tone** in painting. Painters will often talk about the "musical quality" of a painting when its tonal relationships are very much to the fore. Referred to here are the overall effects of colour values and gradations of light and shade. **Harmony** in music, which is a mixing together of separate harmonics or pitches to produce a synthesis, presents us with a useful analogy with **colour**, which mixes together wavelengths of light causing a visual sensation.

Artists use the word **texture** to describe the surface quality of a work of art, whereas musicians use the term more to describe the structural disposition of parts, particularly between the horizontally presented melodic lines and their instrumentation and the vertically presented harmonic blocks. Musical **structure** and visual artistic structure are both understood by comparing the whole and the division of parts of any given work. The word **rhythm** can be equally applied to this relationship of part to part to whole as it can in the microcosm of the movement from one time value to the next. The **balance** of constituents and the use of **contrast** can easily be translated from one art form to the other.

John Paynter's excellent book *Sound and Structure* (1991) sets out a large number of similar advanced composing projects in great detail and will provide years of work for groups of students who can play and notate well.

PROMOTING LISTENING 6

Listening to music is a whole-brain task; it also involves our autonomous system and can engage us in involuntary physical activity. Evidence shows that our feet can be tapping even if no outward movement is perceptible. Our vocal folds move involuntarily when we actively remember a song even if we do not sing it. Our pulses can change according to the stimulus provided by the music. Listening to music can be a profound and beneficial experience, inherent in us but much enhanced by learning. To maximize this learning, choices have to be made.

Just as new library stock must be of good quality, so the aural stimulus chosen by the teacher for their class must also be of good quality, both aesthetically and technically as a recording. It must be able to convey its message in the best possible way to the children. This will depend on several factors, some of them beyond the teacher's control. One is obviously the general state of hearing of the pupils. Increasingly teachers of young children find that deficient hearing is prevalent and affects learning on all fronts. Musical stimulus cannot be fully assimilated unless the sound source is adequate. Many teachers rely on playing tapes to their children in class and give very little regard to the quality of the sound reproduction. If what is employed as a playback machine is a small cassette tape deck normally used by the children themselves for headphone listening, then it is very unlikely that it has the ability to play back enough musical information to make good assimilation possible. The loudspeaker is likely to be tiny and the range of sounds available very small and entirely deficient in some vital areas. A good sound source is vital to the foundation of good music listening skills.

Much musical information played to children will be complex in structure, but the children can pick out salient points. Clear repetitive beats and rhythm patterns, for instance, can be easily recognized. This recognition is considerably advantaged by the teacher helping children to focus clearly upon a single musical aspect and giving that aspect a name. Talking about "steady beat", for instance, is an important early provision of stimulus to encourage the young ear to be focused in its listening and to engage the logical, naming part of the brain in the process of listening alongside the intuitive reception of sounds. Unless sounds are recognized for what they are, the further encoding or comprehension of the musical information cannot so easily proceed. Many of us will have experienced listening to very new music which can challenge our fundamental notions of what music actually is. Such music not uncommonly brings about a state of anxiety and incomprehension in the listener. Without initial sorting and comprehension of the data received we cannot proceed to understanding and retaining that data.

Musical "meaning" and "understanding" is essentially sound-based

Executive functions (i.e. singing, complex rhythmic tasks) are fundamentally dependent on serial temporal and sequential organization and may depend on processing systems that were lateralized very early ...

Trained musicians tend to regard music as an on-going series of interrelated events over longer periods of time ... This perception requires short- and long-term memory, internal perceptual representations, and strategies of temporal organization similar to that we observe in motor skills or verbal syntax. When this in-depth analysis is required, the evidence indicates that trained musicians tend to process music with their dominant hemisphere ...

Thus, it is plausible to hypothesize that in the process of learning musical tasks that involve sequential programmes, analogous to most of language, speech or praxis, there would be an initial tendency to share specialized neural processors with most of the other functions. Thus, the preferential left hemisphere lateralization found in musicians would be due both to the cognitive "linguistic" structure of classical music, the need for their processing along syntactical algorhythms and in general to cognitive operations that imply related computations and prelearned internal representations.

Martin (1982).

Dr Frances Rauscher from the University of California at Irving has led the recent research (1993) into the beneficial effects of playing Mozart to students before they perform cognitive tasks. It was found that, for a limited period of time, their test scores increased significantly.

rather than logic-based. We can comprehend and understand an even series of sounds in time as "steady beat" without ascribing any further referential meaning to it. At the same time in each of us the intensity of such beats, their speed and presentation will bring about some general and some very personal connotations. Most humans, across cultural groups, will find an intensely presented steady beat produces, as well as the understanding of this as a steady beat, an association with and even a feeling of aggression linked to the actual physical effect which such beats have on us. Beyond this general agreement, the nuances of understanding are purely personal and dependent upon the information already stored and available to any one listener. Both sides of the brain cooperate in providing a whole experience of the beat. The left understands it as a beat in time and the right places it in comparison with the norm and feels its effect.

We know, however, that this kind of understanding can be achieved without a teacher. Indeed it would be wrong in general to overemphasize the effect that teachers have on children. Some of the most effective learners are auto-didacts – people who have found out for themselves without any formal tuition. Not enough is known about this process and the motivations which empower it. It is very evident from musical history that auto-didacts such as Wagner, Berlioz and Tippett are as effective in their own right as those composers who received an intensive musical education, such as Bach, Beethoven and Britten. There is much evidence in the music profession at the moment to show that self-taught performers can do equally well in many fields, especially that of vernacular music. Teachers, however, are vital in motivating pupils towards self-teaching, and providing the necessary resources.

The process of understanding can take place only when comprehension is complete, and it is at this stage that the understood data can link into all the other relevant data we have stored. The more interlinking that goes on, the more likely it is that the stimulus is fully appreciated. If the child has experienced "steady beat" in many other musical contexts it is increasingly likely that such interconnections will be made. In stimulating and developing the brain's amazing ability to interconnect lies much of the secret of successful teaching. Until young listeners have comprehended and understood there is little chance of the listening experience being anything more than generally decorative.

The retention or internalizing of musical information takes place once the previous processes have been successful. The more that retained information is referred to, the more effective it will be in recall. Recall is the ultimate goal of the process. If recall does not take place regularly enough, the priority given to the storage of this information is downgraded.

Teachers may observe the beneficial physical and social effect on children of collective listening. Children are often better focused and more amenable immediately after such times. This is reinforced by the research in California at present into the effects of listening to Mozart on students' high-level skills. It also ties in with the evidence from both the specialist music schools in Hungary and the choir schools of Great Britain, where such musically focused education shows a measurable improvement in the expected skills of children in fundamental high-level (non-musical) tasks.

The evidence of all psychological experiments in musical perception over the last decade or so points clearly to the involvement of left-brain skills in trained musicians listening to music or performing musical tasks, whereas non-musicians engage simply the right brain, learning to use the left brain only as the tasks repeat. People trained to use the left brain in right-brain initiated tasks (for example, musicians) appear to show a more adaptable brain use than do those who have been trained only to use the left brain. There is also strong evidence to show that humans are well able to learn to choose which hemisphere to use for a particular task and that the ability to make such a choice can be educated. We have to be able to know how and when to engage what parts of our brain, just as in physical education we have to learn how to engage various muscles.

A PE teacher will work children through a programme of stretching and moving muscles and ligaments, not because the pupils don't use these muscles, but because they have to be increased in capacity and, more importantly, the individual has to become self-aware or body-aware. It is an important part of a training programme to know about and learn to feel the muscle you are exercising, to be conscious of it, and to work it hard, knowing what it does and how and when best to use it. Tony Buzan's work on mental discipline (1989) shows exactly the same attitude. The brain is an organ like any other, and it is important that we understand the essentials of how it works and how we can make use of it to our advantage. The hard work of exercising it then starts, using techniques learnt from others and also finding what suits the individual best. As we have seen, high-level skills can be developed through attentive listening.

Listening to music corporately is a norm, a constant in all societies. It is universally known to be beneficial to the human condition. Social interaction is enhanced by the act and individuals find a high level of communication enhanced between each other. Sympathetic autonomous rhythms are also set up, which can be sensed through very primitive mechanisms similar to the fear mechanisms in animals – the raising of hair on the nape of the neck or the constricting of the diaphragm, and the raising or lowering of the pulse rate. Finger-tip temperature measurements in listening show clearly that when the music is judged to have a high emotional content then there is a consequent involuntary temperature change in all the audience. This kind of sympathetic autonomy can be observed in other social situations where the common stimulus is strong.

Collective listening to music, then, can be socially beneficial, but it is under threat in our society. The invention of the radio, the gramophone, the tape recorder and most pertinently the personal stereo is changing the nature of the experience of listening for the majority of the pupils we teach in Great Britain now. Individual listening, without collective activity, is obviously also pleasurable. It is observable in all strata of our society. Cars have radios, tape decks or CD players. The car is now one of the main concert arenas, and the rapid development of music channels on radio networks all over the world shows how listening in this situation is known to be beneficial. The general effect of the experience would suggest that there is some specific and positive physical effect on us.

Music majors and Computer Science majors use similar cerebral hemispheric dominant and right preferences for problem solving but Music majors are more likely to use an integrated processing mode than Computer Science majors. Computer Science majors are more likely to use left processing mode.

Chesson, D. et al. (1993). "Hemispheric preferences for problem solving in a group of music majors and computer science majors", Instructional Psychology, 20, June.

And it came to pass, when the evil spirit from God was upon Saul, that David took an harp, and played with his hand: so Saul was refreshed, and was well, and the evil spirit departed from him.

1 Samuel 16: 23.

Perhaps the reason why the legends about music, such as Orpheus, suggest that its powers are strong and measurable is because of this physical effect. The Ancient Greeks thought so and categorized and documented this, assigning appropriate scales to conjure up specific moods. The resonance of those theories can be felt today in European folk music. The ancient societies of India codified this, and such codes are still apparent in the traditions and practices of modern Indian folk and classical music. In the Old Testament, Saul's mental illness was calmed by music, and there is strong circumstantial evidence to suggest that the sounds of certain musical instruments have a particularly soothing effect.

The effectiveness of music therapy is strongly proven in modern society, and is increasingly practised, not only with disturbed children and adults but in more general ways, to the benefit of all. There is an obvious link with the sound of strong rhythmic beating and collective physical action. Dancing is the collective and social form of such action and, as such, ameliorates and disperses aggression. Apparently the "war dance" is a Western notion imposed by casually observing intruders into less developed societies. Native Americans will explain that the notion of a frenzied war dance before rushing off to do battle is not one known in their culture, or in any come to that. Indeed dancing is more likely to disperse aggression than to enhance it. Modern society has seen a great increase in provision of places and opportunities to take part in physically heightened dancing. As we advance more into a society which has little formal warring, the outlets for aggressive behaviour become more and more necessary. Heightened physical dancing is the result, and the more sedentary and inactive our young people become the more they feel the need to work off their aggression in dancing. The collective nature of modern disco dancing is interesting since it is undoubtedly collective, but the action for any one participant is entirely individual. In such dancing we enact the problems we find of living in an increasingly dense world population as members of a society which becomes increasingly individualistic as it gets more and more crowded. The collective nature of traditional dancing such as country dancing produces a very different reaction in participants. Organizers of parties for young people know that, if it is possible to involve the young in collective traditional dancing, the party actually goes better. People actually talk to each other more and are more willing to ameliorate their individualistic attitude. Barn dances produce just this sort of effect, and it is fascinating to observe the different results on participants when disco dancing returns during an evening of country dancing; suddenly they stop communicating and become isolated and self-absorbed in their actions.

Formal collective dancing enhances listening to music and maximizes the beneficial physical effect of music on the recipients. The perception of and reaction to pulse, metre, phrase, cadence, strong and weak accents, syncopation and melodic sequence are all enhanced by dancing. Mellers' (1965) theory of the development of Western music, bringing together a synthesis of Agape and the dance, is very pertinent here. The appearance of dance rhythms in Western music synthesized with the spiritually based melodic forms in new forms of music brought about the flowering of musical renaissance. In most forms of music listened to today the synthesis of melody and rhythm bring together brain reactions which go deep into primitive brain structures and stimulate sensori-motor areas at the same time as temporal areas and those areas where emotions are codified.

Listening collectively

As well as being played in the classroom, music can be played formally to larger school groups met together for other purposes. This can affect and be part of the general teaching strategies for schools, but in Great Britain it must also satisfy government guidelines on collective worship. One of the most difficult aspects of the planning of the overall school curriculum is that of the provision of spiritual experience for pupils. In the USA this would be a contentious issue since the government disassociates itself from any religious affiliation. Yet the spiritual needs of children exist in all cultures and countries, and it is part of the caring duty of all schools to be aware of children's needs. The lack of this kind of essential human experience of spiritual things in the present lives of the young in England, Scotland and Wales gravely concerns many people, including the political controllers of our schools' curriculum.

Headteachers and governors are enjoined through the guidelines and statutory aspects of the National Curriculum to provide spiritual experience for children and to inspire in children a sense of awe and wonder. Schools are required to provide opportunity for daily collective worship. A recent government circular directs teachers to provide an opportunity for pupils to experience reverence or veneration paid to a divine being. Teachers in other cultures and countries may find this hard to believe and will sympathize with their British counterparts over the difficulty of such a task. But this area of human experience – feeding the spirit – lies at the heart of the policy of teaching the arts and is a central part of aesthetic experience, which in turn is central to our understanding of and need for the arts. That sense of "encounter" with music described by Keith Swanwick (1988), and for which he rightly claims such a central role, interacts strongly with the sense of otherness we can experience from listening to music either individually or in an audience. Because of the right brain's ability to relate intimately to many other allied areas, and most particularly to help us to provide an integrated image of self, music and the arts have always been associated with spiritual life, from the earliest recorded history of all cultures. That sense of worth which is at the heart of the experience of worship can be accessed through music by many people. Listening collectively or individually, while both provide the possibility of aesthetic experience, is quite different in effect, since collective listening is also capable of producing in the participants a feeling of being linked together by a magic net of the experience. This same feeling of connection through heightened experience is at the heart of all collective worship. Actual physical reaction to the aesthetic experience is heightened in shared listening to music, although it is possible to reproduce these sensations at will as individuals when listening to music in isolation. It is likely that having taken part in effective collective listening prior to concentrated individual listening is essential for access to the full range of experience, although this thesis would be difficult to research and to prove. In a world of individual stereo systems, a new form of listening is growing about which we know very little as educators. Young people – and some not so young –

now listen individually in the street, in the home, on public transport, when driving, cycling or exercising. This new kind of listening is changing the relationship of the receiver to the stimulus and is providing new challenges and concerns for music educators.

Using listening in collective worship in the primary school

Listening as a large school unit when the pupils and teachers are assembled together is a vital part of the strategy for both the individual teacher and the school, and this opportunity, if handled well, is very positive in its effect on the school in general. We are fortunate in Britain to have this opportunity laid down by statute. The overall delivery of the listening area of the music National Curriculum is very difficult for teachers to execute in their own classrooms without such a whole-school strategy. Whole-school policy planning for listening can help teachers to deliver the breadth of experience required of them in their own classrooms. It can also release them from some of the worries about variety of experience within the individual classroom and allow them there to concentrate on those listening experiences which are pertinent to current topics and issues. Cross-curriculum links can be pursued much more readily knowing that other listening experience is being delivered collectively. Inevitably some teachers will ignore or give a very low priority to listening experiences in their own classrooms. Sometimes this will be due to genuine response to the inordinate pressures of curriculum delivery in the primary school classroom. More often it will be caused by the teachers' own ignorance of or antipathy to the musical experience. We have to face up to the fact that there are a great many such teachers in our schools. A whole-school policy for listening will at least make certain that the children unfortunate enough to be taught by such teachers will be given some listening education.

The planning of the listening repertoire for collective worship must be part of a whole-school policy. Headteachers and governors need to be convinced of the benefits of the practice and to realize that the experience needs to be properly framed to be effective in action. When planning content it must be remembered that the collective listening activity will be strange for most pupils and that it will be important to set up the experience in a very positive and non-threatening way. This attitude will need constant renewal, since modern life militates against the reinforcement of such an activity in life outside the school. Few children are used to the focused listening demanded in the past by church or by some voluntary club activities. Even children who are becoming experienced in ensemble playing as musicians will be engaged in a different kind of active listening. Doing something musical while listening to others in performance is a very different kind of listening skill from receiving the whole musical experience in a state of relative physical passivity and mental alertness. From the evidence of many professional musicians we can learn that it is quite possible to be engaged in a high level of critical and collective listening without being caught up at all into a sense of awe and wonder – with an aesthetic experience. The best professional performances are when this kind of professional listening interacts strongly with the individual aesthetic experience of those performing.

Children and staff in a school assembly have to be able voluntarily to give themselves to the listening experience, and negative coercion is unhelpful. Injunctions which are too negatively based on posture and behaviour are likely to damage or invalidate the collective musical experience. Positive attitudes need to be encouraged, as do relaxation and receptiveness. Children also need to be given enough information or incentive towards attentiveness to allow the whole brain to be properly stimulated. Most important is making certain that music is not used in this situation as a cover for other sound or, even worse, as a signal for other activity. Never should music be used as a device to mask the movement of classes away from assembly. It is tempting to use music for this purpose rather as a march might be used by an army platoon, but fortunately children in school are no longer expected to march in time with the musical stimulus (which might actually be beneficial in a limited sort of way), and in any case they move rapidly away from the musical source, whereas an army band marches alongside its troops. Encouraging children to quit when they hear music is antipathetic to the development of focused listening.

A variety of repertoire should be used, but teachers must always have in mind the need for widening the children's experience as well as the enhanced pleasure we all get in repeated experience. Repetitions should happen within the year and within the term, possibly within the week. The English and Welsh National Curriculum for music requires a very comprehensive listening experience which could very well be interpreted as "all music". It is important to keep the music chosen for such public and collective occasions as assemblies out of the area of controversy and to try to match the spiritual (but not necessarily specifically religious) needs of children with the content. Great care must be exercised in the choice of musical examples to be certain that the intended experience is beneficial to children. In this the teacher's own personal and professional judgements must be paramount. Just as it would not be sensible to play large chunks of an opera such as *Salome* or *Elektra* to young children, it is also not sensible to play the latest hit chart numbers with specifically sexual or sub-cultural texts. Teachers can be caught out in this area by being somewhat innocent of the messages inherent in current youth culture hits, whereas the pupils may well be much wiser. While there may be good reasons for using a piece of music which is commercially a current best-seller, a good rule of thumb both for the classroom and for the assembly is to avoid anything in this area. By using such material the teacher makes it difficult for the pupils to concentrate their attention solely on the musical experience. Instead they engage in a conditioned response arising from high-level commercial research, exploitation and the artificial stimulation of sub-cultural behaviour. Although there can be strong philosophical arguments for engaging children only in the music of the here and now, in practice these can bring with them more real problems of behaviour than most teachers either wish to or should engage in.

Choice and length of music will depend very much on the age and background of the children assembled and also teachers' tastes. A vivid short musical experience will have a more long-lasting effect than many a longer one, and the old adage of "three to four minutes or one side of a shellac record" is most probably right both for the children and for the occasion. But this can vary, and with older children the occasional assembly may well be taken up with the playing of an entire piece or movement. The quality of reproduction is also an important feature in making certain that this activity is effective. The sound system used must allow a good range of frequency to be heard by all the pupils present, and it will be important for the teacher to take the time to test this out *in situ* by listening to the playback from the children's position from time to time. Volume can very easily be misjudged, and too little or too much are both antipathetic. The very best form of musical stimulus is that of real live performance. Such performance should be of the best quality available in terms of both the performer and the instrument. School pianos, for instance, are very rarely good enough instruments to provide the right quality of experience. Headteachers will be well advised to consider the high-quality electronic alternatives now available which both stay in tune permanently and can provide many other timbral and electronic advantages. Parents and members of the local community who can play well should be regularly invited into the school to play in assembly and in the classrooms.

Involving the children

It is a very good policy to involve the children themselves in the selection and presentation of the listening selections. Just as it is often an individual teacher's responsibility on a certain day or week to plan and present the assembly, so it is also important to involve their class, or some of the pupils, in the process. Listening examples can be prepared through the choice of that class and the discussion and planning which precedes the assembly will be an important part of that class's music education. The actual presentation can range from a written cue saying what the music is and where it is from, to paintings about the music or writing about it read by the pupils and/or the teacher. Sometimes the music will be that which the pupils of the class have actually invented themselves and which has worked particularly well. It can have arisen from the stimulus of a particular piece of music by a composer which the pupils used as a basis and departure point for their own work, or it may have arisen from many other areas of stimulus, such as a story, a poem, history or geography.

Secondary schools and collective listening in large groups

The assembly of large groups of pupils in many schools has become a merely bureaucratic and administrative opportunity. In this aspect things have changed radically in the last forty years. As schools increased in size so the collective nature of assemblies changed. Christian hymn singing, which was a staple diet for many pupils in pre- and postwar Britain, provided live musical experience in a fundamental musical style which introduced many pupils to the basic laws of harmony and cadence structure through active musical experience. Through this many pupils also engaged in regular part-singing and thus learnt something of the nature of traditional polyphony and homophony. These practices have largely ceased through the continuing secularization of our society and the pressures of multi-cultural understanding. Nothing much has taken its place, despite the strong efforts of many secondary music specialists to continue part-singing through concert-giving and to some extent in the classroom. The change in age-grouping from the more common 11 to 18 schools of the 1950s to the now far more prevalent 11 to 16 has also provided a problem for the encouragement of part-singing experience, since the transition from treble or alto to tenor or bass is a sensitive one, needing encouragement and the provision of a very positive and supportive school attitude to music-making. Some 11 to 16 schools have adopted techniques involving staff and parents to provide the necessary support and positive atmosphere in which immature male voices can be encouraged. On the whole, sixth-form colleges have been less successful in starting up part-singing involving the changing voice. The psychological break between schools provides a difficult barrier, and this has been most successfully overcome by encouraging participation in productions of musicals where the ability to sing is only one of many contributory skills. Carol services do, however, still provide occasions in which pupils willingly engage in singing activities and can yield some of the only experiences outside the music specialist classroom for the encouragement and development of part-singing. Collective listening to music, or listening as a member of an audience, is an experience which should be provided by secondary schools.

Secondary school governors and headteachers are also responsible for the spiritual and moral welfare of their pupils. The sense of awe and wonder is a required whole-school experience, and the secondary school pupil has easy access to this through music. As the brain develops through puberty, particularly the full evolution of the corpus callosum, it is likely that this "sense of awe and wonder" may be felt at full strength for the first time. It has been noted by many observers of religious practice that religious ideas are more accessible – perhaps even more believable – in a musical context than through speech and logical argument. The religious experience of wonder and awe is most likely to emanate from the right hemisphere in conjunction with the right limbic system, with which it is intimately connected. Planning for experiences which actively involve right-hemisphere access is therefore necessary. Recent research has shown that listening to certain types of music involves the left rather more than the right hemisphere, and this places a heavy responsibility of choice on music teachers in secondary schools. It has been shown recently through PET scans and topographical brain mapping that music which is highly atonal or highly "cerebral" in content engages the left hemisphere more than the right in most listeners. Whereas this type of music will take its place in the classroom curriculum for reasons of cultural enquiry and experience, it is likely that music used for large-group collective listening should be biased towards that most likely to inspire the aesthetic response which will most engage the right hemisphere.

The planning of focused listening experiences in secondary assemblies should be undertaken by a team of teachers including the specialists responsible for music and for religious education. Breadth of repertoire and frequency of repetition must be properly taken into account. First listening, that is, listening to music you have never heard before, involves different mental processes from that of second or third listening, and so on. Experience in the category, style or genre of the music is also important to the ability of the listener to decode the messages. There is good evidence now to show that musical memory is one of the first and strongest life experiences and one of the oldest life-

We concluded that the relevant dominance of a hemisphere could indicate how the musical styles of certain composers develop. We realised that mainly intuitive composers, writing essentially emotional music, would use the rhythmic and concordant language of the right hemisphere, where meaning, emotions and rhythm are experienced. Those whose work was predominantly intellectual and logical would draw on the dissonant, arhythmic world of the left.

Robertson (1992).

Despite the fact that music displays itself "in time", the temporal perceptual task of the listener who hears the recurring rhythmic clusters of a popular tune is quite simple: it consists in merely discovering and identifying a musical segment of very short duration that consists of repetition of a rhythmic, melodic or timbral pattern with hardly any harmonic, instrumental, or contrapuntal complexity. Hardly any analysis of the information is needed, and usually the perceptual task is performed well by the right hemisphere …

Martin (1982).

skills we have, ontologically speaking. Musical memory is a given in all of us to a greater or lesser extent, but, like all other mental skills, it has to be nurtured and encouraged.

The process of memory is described by psychologist Tony Buzan (1989) as similar to clearing a path through forest undergrowth. The first time you walk through, a rough track is left behind, and the second and third times allow you to clear out more and more undergrowth and make the pathway easier to walk, providing a quicker journey. The more you repeat patterns of thought, the less resistance there is to them. The easier the journey into those areas of our brain affected by music, the more the aesthetic effect has a chance to operate. Schoenberg once suggested that no new music can possibly be beautiful on first acquaintance. Listening to music is, indeed, something which has to be worked at by the brain, although we must also acknowledge that there is always the possibility of the "instant conversion syndrome". This will depend upon the receptiveness of the receiver and the background of experience brought to the listening. Hans Keller (as quoted in Keith Swanwick's *A Basis for Music Education*, 1979) describes the essential foreground and background experience of the listener. He articulates clearly what was also part of Kandinsky's theory of art appreciation. "Kandinsky's Triangle" describes the interrelatedness among the receiver of art, the maker of art and the art work itself. Even if all we bring to listening to a piece of music is the memory of having heard it before, our attitude towards it will be altered by the existence of that memory, making us more able to make sense of it and to receive some positive aesthetic experience. Enjoyment of music is very much dependent on the ability of the memory to hold information and to recognize patterns and sounds which have been heard before. It also depends on a high level of expectation being raised and gratified. The simpler the patterns, the more instant is the gratification. This goes some way towards explaining why popular music is popular. By "popular" is meant not only currently commercial music retailed through the media, but all those pieces of the listening repertoire which have stuck as favourites. We also know that the gratification is short-lived and that, if the music has a high level of prediction success, we tend to reject the experience. In other words, unless the brain has something else to feed on, something more complex to memorize and predict other than easily assimilated and memorized patterns, we will reject the musical stimulus as being stale.

Many of us also experience the temporary rejection of music which we have listened to so often that we "know" it too well. The normal human reaction is to give such music a rest by not selecting it, thus allowing some forgetting to go on, or at least some distribution of memory stock to a lower access storage system. On return to this music it is often possible to refresh the aesthetic experience in the light of different expectations arising from the use of a different memory base. Often it is important for us to hear new interpretations of old favourites, since a new performer may bring about a whole new set of possibilities and gratifications of prediction.

As in the primary school, the detailed planning and, where possible, delivery of the music used in secondary school assembly should be by the pupils themselves. This must of course be done in discussion with and under the supervision of the specialist teachers. Listening experiences for assembly should be planned well in advance to allow resources to be made available, and to avoid the misappropriation of the experience by opportunist pupils. Part of the appraisal mechanism should be for pupils of all ages to produce an appropriate introduction to a piece of music to be played in assembly. The music may be live or recorded. If live, then the music specialist has an important role to play in making certain that the quality of the listening experience for the majority of the pupils does not suffer in order to encourage or promote a timid or poor performer. It could well be a very interesting task for GCSE pupils to prepare an ideal listening list for a specified term of assemblies, showing how they have met the criteria of the National Curriculum's general requirements. More importantly, they will need to justify their choice of music through arguments on quality and appropriateness to other pupils, to the time of year and to the school's own interests.

Listening in the classroom

A termly listening strategy is necessary, otherwise teachers will find that the day-by-day matters that occupy most of their "on-feet" thinking time will ensure that no organized and progressive listening happens. Playback equipment needs to be available both for the teacher and for the children. Just as in assembly, the act of listening needs to be built into the day as part of the class ritual, and just where this is will depend on the school's, the children's and the teacher's needs. Since corporate listening needs the children gathered together in one place, and there are only a few occasions during an infant's class day when this happens, listening to music for just a minute or so can be built into that gathering in some way, making certain that music isn't merely used as a mask for other noise.

At Key Stage 1 teachers may choose to play one piece of music every day for a week. This would be very good practice since it affords ample repetition, and therefore heightens the interest and pleasure for the children. Short pieces featuring clear instrumental colours, with an emphasis on single instruments, are preferable, and a variety of styles and types of music should be planned over the year, including music from the European classical tradition and that of other world cultures. The identification of the music and composer is relatively unimportant, although teachers may choose to discuss this with the children if they feel that they might gain something interesting and relevant from it. Alternatively the music for the week can be identified by a display card in the music corner, plus perhaps some appropriate visual material. In this case it would be sensible for a copy of the tape to be made available to the children for individual listening by choice, using headphones.

Just as there will be a choice of books in the infant and junior classrooms, so there should be a choice of listening material. Commercially available tapes can be used, but it may also be sensible to make very short single tapes of pieces to provide a choice for the children. Such tapes can be accompanied by a picture code or by written material with older children. Materials can be relevant to topic work or could represent all the music planned to be used for corporate listening for that term.

Another opportunity for listening is associated with the other "carpet time" during the day – story time. The link between music and story with young children has already been explained, and the best model for the teacher to follow would be to emulate a radio broadcast or televised story and to analyse how introductory or epilogue music is used. Some stories can be illustrated with music just like books, particularly those traditional tales that promote music as an essential part of the plot. For example, Jack and the Beanstalk could appropriately feature Celtic harp music and Baba Yaga the music of Mussorgsky's *Pictures from an Exhibition*.

Key Stage 2 teachers need to plan their listening experiences more integrally with their timetabled music slots, allowing for a good spread of the new and some repetition. As in the infants' school, junior classes should have access to a library of recorded music, and those schools which run schemes to encourage parents and children to purchase new books should also consider widening them to include recorded music. Children can be helped to set up an essential listening library over the years which could be equally as important to their development as book fiction.

Listening that derives from a particular topic can be very beneficial just as long as it is genuinely planned as listening experience in its own right. This means providing a time when all the class listens concentratedly to the music more than once and allowing listening to give rise to class discussion – and possibly to extension work in composing and performing. Listening concentratedly can be solely for the pleasure that the music provides – a right-brain experience – but more often children need a focus for their thoughts in order to maintain concentration without any visual stimulus, bringing the left brain into play. Unless a piece has a very specific and identifiable programme, listening for the "story the music tells" may not provide anything more than a stimulus for fantasy that will not engage the left brain very much. To do this, other focus points are needed, such as listening for phrase lengths and comparing their structure, noticing repeated motifs and structures, listening for surprises, for melodies, for specific rhythms and so on. The most common listening focus is that of instrumental identification, but unless this is accompanied by some analysis of why this instrument was chosen to play and what the alternatives might have been and the likely change of effect, there is a danger of encouraging mere check-list listening.

Talking about music in terms of probability and possibility and being aware of the choices made and those rejected by a composer is at the heart of appraisal, which is the term favoured by the English and Welsh National Curriculum. As children progress through Key Stage 2, that is from ages seven to eleven, discrimination should be encouraged through questions about music that do not merely accept the art work as it is, but seek to stimulate thoughts about artistic expression, about interpretation, structure and so on. Comparison of performances of the same piece of music by different artists can be a fascinating exercise in fine discrimination and can help to concentrate the minds of both teacher and pupils on the constituent elements of the music. Learning to discriminate between such elements is, in Reimer's (2/1989) view, the heart of the matter. He points out how easy it is to listen merely for the story or the associations created in the listener's mind; similarly we may concentrate on aspects of performance such as conducting technique, intonation or the acoustic. Neither of these attitudes, the referential or the technical-critical (in his terms), approach the aesthetic core of the music, to be found in the elements, or what Reimer calls "concepts".

There has been a long academic debate about the use of the term "concept" – one to which Keith Swanwick takes exception. In *Music, Mind and Education* he states, "the danger with 'concepts' is that we tend to work from them and to them, looking for music which exemplifies their characteristics. This can diminish whatever prospect there may be for musical encounters in the classroom." This insight into the dangers of a "check-list" mentality, true as it is, appears to be based mostly on the experience of specialist music teachers in secondary schools, whereas the generalist primary teacher who approaches music alongside the plethora of other things in the curriculum may well find such a concentration on intrinsic constituents a real toehold. For younger children it is important to provide sign-posts and to help them to discover, to analyse and to discriminate between things. To do this the teacher must try to isolate cogent areas of information in music, and this factual information balances the more subjective area of listening, engaging both sides of the brain. It encourages us, when listening, to be prepared for what might happen and to be pleased when it does and surprised when it doesn't .

As we move up the age-ranges, it becomes increasingly important to encourage a more integrated listening panorama, building on the previous "concept"-based work and accepting that pupils have some powers of discrimination and analysis. The experience of music as an expressive art form is the central issue. Key Stage 3 teachers should continue and extend primary practice, increasingly engaging the class in scan-reading to reinforce left-brain analysis, at the same time concentrating on how the constituent elements of music are used to produce widely differing styles and effects. The exploration of genres, styles and cultures should continue, with chosen examples being more complex in texture, length or style. Listening work needs to reinforce comparison and contrast between musical styles and cultures, particularly emphasizing similarities and noting differences. The music of a classical Indian sitarist can be compared usefully with, let's say, a solo cello suite of Bach, or the gamelan of Indonesia with music of Debussy, Ravel, Orff or Britten. As in the primary school, music whose focus is primarily in a declared subject matter should be approached, in discussion, through the structure of the music itself and its expressive force, and not through identifying the subject matter at the outset.

Key Stage 3 should witness an exploration of the major genres and structures of traditional and classical European music, from the jig, reel, Morris dance and ballad, through to opera, oratorio, concerto and symphony. Classes by the end of this key stage should have experienced polyphony of various types, including fugue and common dance forms such as the minuet. The best experiences will always be found through strategies that link listening with doing in some way, either performing or composing or both. The whole matter of tonality and scales should arise from planned listening, giving experience in whole-tone and modal scales as well as straightforward major and minor. Atonality should also be experienced and discussed, together

The purpose of music education, as Kodály frequently emphasized, should be to help individuals to develop their aesthetic experience and understanding by exercising their powers of discrimination.

Blacking (1987).

Surprise is the privilege only of prepared minds – it takes preparation to discern what is trivially improbability and what is effective surprise.

Bruner, J. S. (1967). The Conditions of Creativity in Contemporary Approaches to Creative Thinking. New York: Atherton Press.

The aim of music in schools must not be to reinforce tribal boundaries or to encourage tokenism by concentrating on pop music in predominantly "working class" schools, reggae in schools with children of Caribbean origin, or Urdu folk-songs where there are majorities of Pakistanis. It is not the business of music educators to subvent community activities, which already exist, or to encourage cultural brokers to mobilize new social groups for social, political, or religious purposes. Music education should not be used to emphasize culture, because as soon as that happens there arise arguments about cultural hegemony, as well as false notions of what culture is: it should emphasize *human* variety and ingenuity.

Blacking (1987).

with some notion of the formal structures that accompany this area. The comparison of performances of pieces of music by different performers, arrangers or conductors should form an important strand in the planning. By the time a pupil arrives by choice at the concentrated focus of an examination syllabus, those studies should be able to delve deeply into detail or the outer fringes of styles and genres, taking the overall breadth of listening experience for granted.

In higher education, students at the beginning of their courses need to be set up with good habits of listening, since the exploration will be largely individual. It is rarely enough merely to allow this to happen if the student is sufficiently motivated, and, particularly in first year courses, listening assignments with real exploratory work need to be planned in all areas of the curriculum, from musicology and analysis through to composition and, most particularly, performance, where comparative performances should be analysed both live and from recordings. Higher education students need to be presented with strategies by teachers that will encourage them to strengthen right-brain and whole-brain approaches that often, by this stage, have become dull and can appear inappropriate. One of the most useful strategies is to engage in the "What comes next?" game, which presents the score of a piece only up to a certain point. Students are then challenged to improvise alternative strategies of continuation that are finally compared with the composer's own solution.

Other possibilities are to set assignments based on listening that require the student to write about what they have listened to from viewpoints that encourage whole- or right-brain thinking. One technique is to ask the student, having first listened through the appointed piece or extract, to write down any words, particularly adjectives, that come into their heads. The list of words collected after several repeated listenings is then turned into a piece of prose or poetry. A further challenge is then to take the prose or poem and to set it to music and perform it.

On a more mundane level, students can be asked to review the piece they have listened to as if they had just attended the first performance. This can be a good exercise in stylistic writing and journalism, both in the historical sense, if an old piece is used, or in the varying styles of contemporary journalism, from *Tempo* and *Classical Music Weekly* through the quality papers to *Melody Maker* and *New Musical Express*. The crux of good teaching of listening in higher education, just as in the other stages, is in discussion, and students can often be purposefully inarticulate. Inarticulacy about music in a music student must be challenged, and teachers should object to all sloppy and undigested terminology, at the same time constantly encouraging and stimulating debate about music. Students should be urged to explore those things that first motivated composers to write, and analytical listening seminars should include study of poetry used by composers, literature of the period where obvious links can be made, paintings, sculpture and architecture. My experience is that students even need to be challenged on basic geography, since there is nothing more arid than the mutual exchange of ignorance that starts with a student's litany of "So-and-so was born in such-and-such a town in such-and-such a country". For this to be of any relevance we need to know something of the history, the political situation and even the climate. All these matters can be focuses for exploration through assignment, encouraging students throughout their privileged years of higher education to link facts together in an ever-increasing network and to become habitual explorers.

New technologies are constantly enlarging our horizons, and the invention of the CD-ROM has provided one of the most exciting new opportunities for the development of listening skills in students of all ages. Although some of the early programmes released on CD-ROM did nothing more than transfer the pages of a book plus an accompanying cassette onto the computer screen, within a short space of time the potential of interactivity to enhance musical learning was already being discovered. There is no other medium that can provide an immediate link in real time between music and the visual, either through word, diagram or illustration, together with choice and interactivity with the user. The techniques already learnt through television are now beginning to find their real home in this new medium. New programmes are being issued regularly, but the excellent deconstruction and guide to Stravinsky's *Rite of Spring* by Robert Winter (1985) and Peter Gabriel's *Xplora* (1994), which gives access to music and instruments from many cultures as well as insight into studio and composing techniques in our vernacular style, are excellent starting-points. All students in upper secondary schools and higher education music departments should have easy access to such materials.

The assessment of listening skills, as in other areas, should involve the student in the process from Key Stage 2 onwards. At Key stage 1 it is enough for the teachers to record each child's interest expressed not only in their comments made in discussion but also in the amount each child has used materials provided for individual listening. By the time children have some reading skill, their listening skills can be tested through simple question sheets accompanying individual listening tapes. At key stages 2 and 3 such strategies can continue, and evidence from "What Do You Hear?" worksheets can also be fed in. This form of linking of words and listening in a carefully focused worksheet was first invented by Richard Colwell for Silver Burdett in the United States, and these materials are available in the British Silver Burdett materials. Most important is the principle that governs them, which is one of listening for information and making decisions about music heard. Worksheets are linked to specifically chosen recorded examples that are carefully numbered, and multiple choice answers are provided, reducing the writing skills required for success, although other types of more open questions can equally well be used. Key Stage 3 pupils should be able to write personal appraisals following class discussions, based on note-taking during the class session. Teachers must make clear to their pupils what the criteria for assessment of such work will be, based on accuracy, fact and well-justified personal opinion.

At Key Stage 4 and beyond, listening diaries and common-place books can help to encourage the essentially personal exploration needed for success in students who have chosen to specialize, and these can form part of an assessment scheme alongside assignments such as those suggested above in the sections covering these age-ranges. Much of the assessment of such courses will be governed by the techniques of examination to which the courses are leading, and there should obviously be careful correlation between assignments, the final examinations and their assessment.

Resumé

- Listening to music is a profound and beneficial experience which is inherent in us but it is much enhanced by learning. Musical stimulus cannot be fully assimilated unless the sound source is adequate.

- Recognition is considerably advantaged by the teacher helping children to focus clearly upon a single musical aspect and giving that aspect a name. Without initial comprehension of the data received we cannot proceed to understand and retain that data. Both sides of the brain cooperate in providing a whole experience in listening.

- The more interlinking of information that goes on, the more likely it is that the stimulus is fully appreciated. Recall is the ultimate goal of the process. Teachers may observe the beneficial physical and social effect on children of collective listening.

- People trained to use the left brain in right-brain initiated tasks (for example, musicians) appear to show a more adaptable brain use than do those pupils who have been trained to use only the left brain.

- Collective listening to music is beneficial in education, but collective listening is under threat in our society. Individual listening, without collective activity, is obviously also pleasurable.

- There is an obvious link with the sound of strong rhythmic beating and collective physical action. Formal collective dancing enhances listening to music and maximizes the beneficial physical effect of music on the recipients.

- One of the most difficult aspects of the planning of the overall school curriculum is that of the provision of spiritual experience for pupils. That sense of worth which is at the heart of the experience of worship can be accessed through music by many people. Listening collectively or individually, while both provide the possibility of aesthetic experience, is quite different in effect, since collective listening is also capable of producing in the participants a feeling of being linked together by a "magic net" of the experience.

- Listening as a large primary school unit when the pupils and teachers are assembled together is a vital part of the strategy for both the individual teacher and the school. Whole-school policy planning for listening can help teachers to deliver the breadth of experience required of them in their own classrooms. The planning of the listening repertoire for collective worship must be part of a whole-school policy.

- Positive attitudes need to be encouraged, as do relaxation and receptiveness. Children also need to be given enough information or incentive towards attentiveness to allow the whole brain to be properly stimulated. Most important is making certain that music is not used in this situation as a cover for other sound or, even worse, as a signal for other activity. Great care must be exercised in the choice of musical examples to be certain that the intended experience is beneficial to children. In this the teacher's own personal and professional judgements must be paramount.

- Just as it is often an individual teacher's responsibility on a certain day or week to plan and present the assembly, so it will also be important to involve their class, or some of the pupils, in the process.

- Collective listening to music, or listening as a member of an audience, is an experience which should be provided by secondary schools. The planning of focused listening experiences in secondary assemblies should be undertaken by a team of teachers including the specialists responsible for music and for religious education. Breadth of repertoire and frequency of repetition must be properly taken into account. As in the primary school, the detailed planning and, where possible, delivery of the music used in secondary school assembly should be by the pupils themselves.

- Just as in assembly, the act of listening needs to be built into the day as part of the infants' class ritual. Listening can be linked with "carpet" activities most helpfully.

- Individual listening facility is also desirable in the infants' classroom, and such facility should continue into Key Stage 2, where planned listening features more strongly in timetabled music slots.

- Topic-linked listening must be treated as a music education experience and not merely allowed to become decorative. Children at this stage need to be increasingly engaged in analysis of what they hear.

- Key Stage 3 teachers continue and extend this practice, increasingly engaging the class in scan-reading to reinforce the left-brain analysis, and should promote an exploration of the major genres and structures of traditional and classical European music.

- In higher education, students at the beginning of their courses need to be set up with good habits of listening, since the exploration will be largely individual. They also need to be presented with strategies by teachers that will encourage them to strengthen the right-brain and whole-brain approaches that often, by this stage, have become dull and can appear inappropriate.

- New technologies are constantly enlarging our horizons, and the invention of the CD-ROM has provided one of the most exciting new opportunities for the development of listening skills in students of all ages.

- The assessment of listening skills, as in other areas, should involve the student in the process from Key Stage 2 onwards. By the time children have some reading skill, their listening skills can be tested through simple question sheets accompanying individual listening tapes. Key Stage 3 pupils should be able to write personal appraisals following class discussions, based on note-taking during the class session. At Key Stage 4 and beyond, listening diaries and common-place books can help to encourage the essentially personal exploration needed for success.

Teaching implications

Listening lessons have to be prepared carefully and attention must be paid to the provision of appropriate support materials. The teacher needs to have listened attentively to the example and to have formed some opinions as well as decided on a factual analysis appropriate to the children's perceptual level. The principle of engaging the ear before the eye is still very much to the forefront.

Example 1: An upper Key Stage 2 class is engaged in a historical study of the Tudors

Lesson focus: Music in late medieval and Renaissance England
Resources: Recordings, copies of "Greensleeves", words of the "Agincourt Song", picture of King's College Chapel, Cambridge, William Byrd's *La Volta*, picture of Elizabeth I dancing the volta.

To demonstrate Tudor court music in the early Renaissance the teacher plays William Byrd's *La Volta*, showing a picture of Queen Elizabeth performing the volta and being lifted into the air by her partner. In contrast to the earlier linear battle hymn and strongly melodic song, *La Volta* is metrical and full of dance rhythms. The teacher draws the class's attention to the inverted rhythm pattern at the end of each four-bar phrase, which indicates the jump into the air, considered so daring in those days. The transition from the decoratively linear to the symmetrical and rhythmic demonstrates in music the transition from medieval to Renaissance, Plantagenet to Tudor.

The class is first introduced to Tudor music through learning the song "Greensleeves". Children who play the recorder have had a part provided for them in advance and the song is sung to the recorder accompaniment. The teacher leads the class in a discussion of the difference between a single-line song accompanied by the same single line on recorders and modern songs with accompaniments using many instruments. The teacher identifies "Greensleeves" as a folk-song and discusses with the class the meaning of this term.

The "Agincourt Song" dates from the Plantagenet dynasty, who were overthrown by the Tudors in 1485 at the end of the Wars of the Roses. Although, like "Greensleeves", the "Agincourt Song" is a single-line melody and no one knows who wrote it, the contrast between this and "Greensleeves" is next discussed by the class, having heard it played to them. The class is asked which piece is the older ("Agincourt Song", 1415). "Greensleeves" is more metrical and with balanced phrases that suggest its having been composed a good hundred years later. The complex line of the "Agincourt Song" is compared with the complex lines of tracery in King's College Chapel. The melody of the "Agincourt Song" is more complicated in structure and does not have such obviously matching phrases. Although it has a metre, this is less apparent than in "Greensleeves" and doesn't sound like music you could dance to. The class is shown the words of the "Agincourt Song" and, in reading through them with the teacher, discovers that it tells a story, is celebratory and martial in atmosphere. The teacher explains that it is very similar to church music and, indeed, is a kind of victory hymn. It was most likely written by one of Henry V's composers of the Chapel Royal. The teacher explains that the two types of music, that for the royal court and that for the ordinary people, are typical of the Tudor period. It is also explained to the class that, since the writing down of music only first became regularized at about the period of Henry V, not a great deal of similar folk and court music survives from before that time, but many of the folk-songs we still sing today were first invented in the late medieval period.

Compare and contrast techniques

Compare and contrast tasks have been used in examination questions for many years. The intentions behind such questions are to encourage the exploration of materials by finding out what is common and what is not and, by doing so, isolating those essential elements that are peculiar to a particular composer, work, genre and style. They encourage the examinee to steer clear of overinsistence on factual detail for its own sake. Most importantly, they help to focus students' attention on the qualities of the music as opposed to, for instance, another common question, "Write short notes on the following works ...", which encourages factual reply. Compare and contrast questions ask for some estimation from students; they encourage them to search for analogous and heterogeneous relationships between things. Examination questions should be able to be seen as microcosms of lessons or lesson sequences. The following "compare and contrast" lesson is based on ideas of Larry Eisman (1968), and explores this technique by helping students of Key Stage 3 age to discover the essential elements of the Baroque style.

Example 2

Lesson focus: To learn the essential attributes of Baroque music
Resources: Playback and tapes, musical examples in notation, OHP

slides of Canaletto's London, a building of modern period, a Baroque building and a well-known local building

The lesson begins with a short extract of Baroque music being played while the teacher projects a coloured overhead projector slide of a detail from a Canaletto view of the Thames in the eighteenth century for the class to see as they listen. The detail shows architecture, costume and transport. The lesson begins by engaging ear and eye, helping to provide the essential stimulus for the right brain.

As the music fades the teacher asks the class to look for the clues that tell them what period of history they might be concentrating on. This open questioning encourages guessing and estimating and a problem-solving attitude. The teacher accepts the answers given but asks each answerer to expound the factual evidence upon which their guess is founded. These facts are recorded on the left side of the board or chart, and the guesses on the right. Open questions can easily be abused by inattentive pupils who give random answers, but this is dealt with by the teacher being insistent upon evidence. Producing evidence moves the task from "gut reaction" to fact, from conjecture, through investigation to some sort of proof. The movement between intuitive thought and cognitive process is an important key to understanding the process of the lesson.

Next the teacher moves into one element of visual evidence raised, for example, architecture, and continues the compare and contrast exercise. Visual evidence is easier to pin down than aural evidence, and this preparatory exercise brings the pupils a little nearer to using evidence and logics in assessing aural evidence. Collecting visual evidence also stimulates responses through spatial, colour and design elements rather than words, stimulating a balance between areas of thinking. Two slides are shown simultaneously, or two posters are displayed. One shows a building not of the Baroque, well known to the class, and the other a building of the Baroque period, also preferably known to the class. The class is then asked to decide what elements are the same in both buildings and in what ways they differ. A further list is built up by the teacher of "same" and "different". All buildings tend to have floors, walls, doors and windows, for instance, but decoration, proportion and materials will be different.

The next task produces a parallel in music which moves the class into a more intangible form of evidence-collecting based only on aural information. This challenges musical memory and examples need to be kept reasonably short. Because the element of time now challenges the memory's retentiveness, pupils are encouraged to make notes about the responses they will have at the end of the two examples. The class is told that there will be two playings through of both pieces in the same order. As they listen, pupils are asked to write down any facts they can identify about the music as single words or phrases. The two musical examples are played; one is a piece of music already familiar to the class carrying a good deal of known information available to the pupils. It should preferably match in period the first illustration of a building. The second is a typical example of Baroque music – a movement from Handel's *Music for the Royal Fireworks*, for instance. Before the class discusses the examples they are asked to sort their information into "same" and "different" headings. A discussion led by the teacher follows and a composite list is drawn up.

By symbol, Peirce meant a sign that derives its meaning from its relationships in a network with other signs. Where musical signs are indexical or iconic, the meaning can often be read from the sign directly – as with thunder and the pitter-patter of raindrops in Beethoven and Rossini, or even the firm footsteps of faith in Bach. The meaning of musical symbols arises from their place in the syntax of a piece and, more broadly speaking, of a style. ... A symbol thus depends for its significance on its place in the musical pattern in relation to other symbols. ... The essentials of Mandler's theory of emotion are as follows: human cognition operates by means of perceptual-motor schemata through which (largely unconscious) expectancies are generated for upcoming events and by which future behaviours are planned. The interruption of an ongoing schema or plan brings about biological arousal – a signal that something is gone wrong. This reaction in turn triggers a search for a cognitive interpretation of what happened – a search for meaning. The arousal and interpretation join together in producing an emotional experience of a particular quality ...

Dowling and Harwood (1986).

Next the class is issued with sheets containing a musical example from the Baroque period which has been chosen in order to engage the pupils as performers. The choice of example will vary according to the performing skills of the children, but a good choice would be something with a strong and simple melodic element which can be sung and played both by itself and together with the recording. Bach's "Wachet Auf" chorale would be such an example, or Pachelbel's *Canon*. The class learns to perform the example from the teacher's arrangement. Differing aptitudes and skills can be accounted for in separate tasks, and the given examples provide both simple and more complex lines.

Having performed the example and integrated the performance with a recorded performance, either by listening or by playing along, the pupils have their attention focused on the strong melodic elements in both treble and bass lines. Using short extracts, each line is isolated in turn for the pupils to hear them as single elements, and then combined. If possible, pupils are asked to perform both of these, at their own pitch, by singing or playing along with the line. The teacher reinforces to the class that one of the major identifying elements of Baroque music is the constant interaction between treble and bass lines. Other elements such as repeated patterns, sequences, driving regular pulse, constant metre, instrumentation and polyphonic texture are discussed with the class and are recorded by both pupils and teacher.

An easily commissioned follow-up task could be a short written account of the main elements of Baroque music using the notes collected in the lesson. A prompt sheet issued by the teacher would increase the element of differentiation. A more far-reaching task would be to repeat the core of the lesson with two new pieces of music, available on a message tape, together with a prepared sheet of questions of a "compare and contrast" type. The more difficult task can be used when the circumstances allow or demand a more challenging approach. The availability of playback has to be considered plus the cost of message tapes and the time it takes to make extract recordings. Teachers who organize their classes to allow a variety of musical activities to take place at once will be better able to use the more far-reaching task, since it will involve only a sub-set of pupils using equipment and materials, while others are differently engaged in related tasks.

This lesson provides good stimulus to both cognitive and affective thinking processes. It stimulates problem-solving attitudes and provides the basis for techniques in this area when listening to unknown music. It establishes enough facts about the music to allow pupils to write about the task using information that will encourage musical memory while avoiding extraneous and unnecessary historical or biographic details that carry no musical sound memories with them. By linking technical words clearly with the sounds they represent, words, phrases, musical notation and pictures all have the possibility of awakening in the pupils' memories the sounds that gave rise to them. The process of sounding symbols is at work …

INSTRUMENTAL TEACHING

The physical and technical demands of each instrument are different. For example, flutes and trumpets need work on embouchure, whereas piano needs more attention to fingering and coordination, cellos need bowing, and so on. We can be so caught up in the specialisms and the acquisition and progression of motor skills demanded by the instrument that, as teachers, we too easily ignore the shared basic principles of instrumental teaching. These lie in the development of an individual musical response in students, giving them problem-solving skills which enable them to continue to learn and develop with positive self-criticism away from the teacher for the rest of their lives.

In the initial lessons, teachers of beginners must inevitably focus very largely on establishing posture and correct physical attributes. It is vital that enough attention is given to the ease and comfort of young players and that they feel at one with their instrument before they attempt anything physically demanding. There is a temptation for some teachers, often urged by the enthusiasm of the pupils themselves, keen to advance, to skimp on this foundation laying, dealing with it largely at the outset and after that only intermittently. Suzuki violin teachers approach this in a very structured way by ensuring that pupils are entirely at ease with the unnatural and awkward posture and holds. Before pupils even graduate to a small size instrument, they use a scrap material instrument, involving them first in imaginative play. It may be several months before pupils are presented with real instruments. Fundamental movements that are integral to the particular instrumental performance are established using the model instrument, while pupils listen to the sounds they should be making. These are played by the teacher and, from the first, children build up aural memories of good practice as they establish psychomotor routines that will, with luck, become second nature to them. However a teacher chooses to establish beginning practice, good, healthy and effective psychomotor skills must be secured at the outset.

At the heart of this development, alongside that of building strong psychomotor skills, is the establishment of an analytical and acute musical ear coupled with a creative approach to interpretation, reinterpretation and invention. The reading of notation is for many Western musicians a necessary skill, but overreliance on notation can be inimical to aural development and to a problem-solving approach to performing. It can also dissuade many students from developing the enormous potential of their long-term musical memory. Many performers who graduate from their instrumental programmes in Britain have fallen into this complicated trap.

We must also be open to the highly successful and centuries-old teaching and learning traditions of musicians of cultures all over the world. Western methodology has produced performing musicians who

Beginning performers, no matter what their age, will have to be engaged quickly in decision-making responsibilities. The very first lessons, whether individual or group, will have to include opportunities to use, in imaginative musical ways, whatever sounds the performers can make at that point.

Reimer (2/1989).

Dr S. Suzuki's *Talent Education* movement began in 1945, and has involved many Japanese preschoolers in learning to play miniature, scaled-down violins. Suzuki expresses the fundamental belief that musical talent can be nurtured in any child, drawing an analogy with the learning of natural language. Since children very skilfully and rapidly learn their mother tongue at an early age, he argues that learning instrumental skills should also begin in the first few years of life.

A vital part of the method is the involvement of the mother, who also learns the violin herself in the early stages. … The curriculum is based on playing by ear rather than on reading notated music, and success at each stage is evaluated in terms of the accuracy of the pupil's reproduction of model performances. There is a strong emphasis on memory training, imitation, and repetition.

Hargreaves (1986).

... the written page should be discarded and the music committed to memory. Only then will music be realised internally and the musician play directly from his imagination. Written notation, like everything else in this complex age, is a literal fact that tends to cover up live reality, and in the end is only a vehicle that has to be discarded to move into a new dimension.

Whone, H. (1976). *The Integrated Violinist.* London: Gollancz.

have become influential internationally partly because of the development and sophistication of communications systems in their society. The growing dominance of all forms of Western music worldwide must also be ascribed somewhat to the virtues of the art forms it contains, the skills that sustain it, and their ability to communicate with many different people. But there are many worrying aspects of Western musical culture, none more so than the threat to mental and physical health that high-level performing of Western music can become. Part of this is due to the intensity of the demands of the modern life-style of professional musicians, but some can be traced to the initial methods of musical education of performers. At the slightly lower level than the top-flight performers, we have too many professional and good amateur players who do not function as well as they would like as all-round musicians. Some of this is due to the dominance of printed notation that, from the very first lessons, can adversely affect our posture and mental set.

The emphasis on sight-reading from music notation is at a premium in our society. It is far more in focus in Great Britain even than it is in other European countries, although this obsession is of a more general Western European origin. British children and adults are required to sing and to play at sight to a very high level. They are constantly submitted to rapidly changing repertoire and demanding performances given with the minimum of rehearsal. Whether we are talking about orchestral musicians, string quartet players, choral society members, cathedral choristers or army bandsmen, all are constantly on the move, absorbing, digesting and discharging repertoire at an enormous rate. Once a thing is performed it is over and they are on to the next piece.

If we follow the musical life of many children in school who have orchestral instrumental lessons from an early age we can see a typical model of development. The first years of learning are spent as individuals playing from notation from the initial lesson. The teacher functions largely as observer and critic and conveys information verbally. It may be several years before pupils play in public. After the initial individually taught introductory period, sometimes of several years, children then may also join an ensemble. Depending on the quality and demand of this ensemble, sight-reading suddenly becomes the greatest imperative. Running with the pack at their speed is necessary and much repertoire is played through, often in a less than satisfactory way for the individual. This applies particularly to those people who play instruments such as violins or cornets, where they are one of many.

A great deal of pleasure and skill will be gained from this experience and a wide repertoire knowledge. Concerts will be given in stimulating environments, sometimes in other countries. At the end of this the adult emerges who has a true dedication to music and who is able to play and to sight-read well in, say, the local *Messiah* or more ambitious projects, join the local symphony orchestra and so on. The practice of their musicianship, however, is most likely to be limited to sight-reading and their ability to function as musicians in society away from the notation is limited, sometimes non-existent. They are unable and unwilling to improvise and need the discipline imposed by others, conductors and so on, to be able to function well. They cannot originate musical ideas of their own and find it difficult to create their own new interpretations of existing music, needing the continuing advice of teachers.

Most worrying, often their aural acuity is weak and both tone quality and fine intonation poor. One area of the performing personality has been developed at the expense of others. Put such a musician at a social function and ask them to use their musical skills and they are lost. Go to such a musician and ask them to play a melody recently heard on the radio, and they are unable to do so. Ask such a musician to accompany a dance, play a lullaby, a march, cheer us up with music, provide sweet music for the soft lights and the answer is always the same, "I would if I had my music …"

There are other models of practice in British society which are worth our attention. The musical life of a cathedral chorister provides a good contrast to that of the individual instrumentalist (although choristers are often instrumentalists as well). The cathedral musical tradition stems from Western European medieval practice which has survived in Britain but is largely lost in other countries; it remains one of the real jewels in our national musical crown. It is one of the few survivals of music education practice from our cultural past and, as such, provides us good ontological evidence for what works best in good practice.

Working always through the voice develops in the child a very different set of essential musical skills, which are totally focused on an acute ear and good memory. Singing different polyphonic service settings each day, including florid anthems in a wide variety of musical periods and styles, these young musicians digest material at a phenomenal rate. Choristers are hardly taught formally to sight-read – they just have to do it to survive, and their first experience is not of sight-reading laboriously, note by note, but that of scan-reading. Their survival as a chorister depends on an intensively working musical memory with notation acting as a memory aid.

Their short-term musical memory is honed to perfection, motivated initially by fear as much as by enthusiasm for music, and very quickly the dots and lines begin to make some kind of overall sense. Certain well-tried pieces of repertoire do come round again and eventually become very familiar and committed to the long-term musical memory, but mostly the chorister is performing new things and is under considerable stress to achieve perfection. The combination of memory, aural alertness and gradually growing reading skills all based on the voice provides one of the most superb foundations for continuing musical practice.

The teaching methods of cathedral choir-trainers can produce amazing results and should be closely studied by all choral conductors. Because the essential skills are vocal, all the focus of attention is on the development of the ear and on the achievement of a particular kind of sound which goes with it. A young probationer chorister learns most from his next-door neighbour. A good deal of miming goes on in the first weeks and months and much is learnt through close imitation. The results are at a consistently high level and continue to provide us with some of the best free concerts of choral music available anywhere in the world.

In a choristers' rehearsal there is always preparatory technical exercise which feeds directly the required tone quality of the choir. Each choir sounds different even though the raw materials are roughly the same from place to place. The choir-trainer places a personal stamp on them through exercise of technique using traditional methods of sung scales and arpeggio figures. This is achieved not in individual lessons but within a group of twenty or so at a time. However, each individual's progress is noted carefully by the choir-trainer. Sometimes faults are acknowledged by the children themselves by a voluntary raising of the hand when they know they have gone wrong. Everything is achieved by a mixture of quick thinking, doing and feeling, with the strong incentives of high expectation and public exposure. Throughout the rehearsals, the choir-trainer plays and sings, modelling all the procedures and leading the way towards subtlety of musical expression by example – not necessarily through perfection of voice, for some choir-trainers are poor vocal executants – but through using music itself to convey musical ideas.

No time is wasted, since it is at a premium, and the whole period is spent in rehearsing, fault-finding and acknowledging, refining and expanding musical experience. In cathedrals this will happen at least once every day in term time, and it could well be pointed out that, given such regular rehearsal, no one could possibly fail to improve. However, excellent results are also achieved by large parish church choirs whose rehearsals are more likely to be twice a week and an hour before a service. Considering the amount of repertoire covered it is remarkable that such choirs not only fulfil their office duties but also prepare large concert works to perfection.

Although improvisation is likely to be a weakness there is far more chance that an ex-choral scholar will have a creative approach to music-making; however, there is not too much documentary evidence to demonstrate this. Many ex-choral scholars go on to become practising composers and performers. There is certainly some evidence to show that such an early training stimulates all high-order skills, not just musical ones. Overall educational results are known to be better from choir schools than those achieved in similar schools without this particular form of music education.

There are essential differences between the two models of instrumental teaching that I have described. The choral "lesson" is normally taught in a large group, and the instrumental lesson in a small group or with individuals. There is a clear musical end-product from the choral lesson and the incentives to learn quickly which go with it provide high motivation. The musical outcome of an instrumental lesson is more often vague. The isolation of individual instrumentalists can help some students by protecting them from exposure but it can, by the same token, be demotivating. The technical exercises in the choral rehearsal develop the instrument, and, at the same time, both the ear and tone quality. The teacher teaches constantly through musical stimulus by performing him- or herself. The instrumental teacher (and, ironically, it can be one and the same person) too often teaches not through performing but only through comment and critique. Technical exercises can be divorced from aural development and are rarely considered to be essentially sound-focused.

As a stereotypical example of individual instrumental teaching, let's now examine a piano lesson with a well-established pupil in some detail. Lessons can vary in length between a half and a whole hour, giving less time than the choir-trainer has, but without any of the immediate demands of constant public performance and consequent breadth of repertoire. Like the choral rehearsal, the lesson will traditionally begin with exercises, often scales and arpeggios. These exercises are essential in setting up a memory-bank of applicable movement-based procedures. Unlike the choir, the piano student can perform these exercises without needing to engage the musical ear; in fact such exercises are often approached by not engaging any musical judgement at all. Since their performance is solo, the pacing does not depend on anyone else, as it would in a group. The element of performance is lacking here. There is often no perceived need for expression or phrasing, no attention to tone colour and not much to speed and articulation. These would appear to be superfluous to the learning required, which is largely sensori-motor.

What is often more worrying, these scales and arpeggios can stand isolated in an area of learning unattached to anything. To the student they may appear an end in themselves and are practised as such. The choice of scale is often set out in a printed tutor, worked out by finger pattern or harmonic systems and facilitating ease of approach for the player. This technical part of the lesson is obligatory and unengaged in feeling response or problem-solving. It is often treated "medicinally" as something relatively unpleasant to be surmounted and dismissed. There is rarely any planned application of any of the learning gained to any immediate musical context or to the activities that follow. More often than not, the pupil makes the choice of the exercises to be played. It is common to hear teachers say to students, "Which ones shall we do next?" There is some interesting evidence from McGill University showing, through use of PET scans, that musicians playing scales do not engage the right brain through which sound is processed. They use only the left brain, which understands logics, for this is all that is required. However, when a student meets the same scale disguised as a figure or motif in a piece, it needs expression, articulation, mood, rubato, etc., and none of the controls for these are available in the left brain.

Scales and arpeggios are most often learnt from notation and gradually committed to the long-term memory after a long and hard process of repeated action. Once securely there, they are available for application to new musical contexts. The process by which this happens is not yet really understood, but there appears to be a considerable problem of retrieval for many students in matching up and selecting appropriate finger patterns and applying them to new musical contexts in a musical way. Scales and arpeggios learnt as isolated patterns and not experienced as "gestalts" through problem-solving will not be so easily deconstructed for application in new circumstances.

The next phase of the lesson is often given over to the playing of studies. Studies place technical problems in a quasi- and sometimes whole-heartedly musical context, and this is a positive process which moves the pupil nearer to the real task of performing. The playing of studies should involve the whole musical brain, but more often this too engages only the logics, as with scales. Both teacher and pupil could be helpfully employed in inventing studies pertinent to an individual's needs, and whenever composers have been instrumental teachers this

The major, most serious, most debilitating errors in performance instruction are (1) to separate skills from their musical uses; (2) to so overemphasize skills, especially at the beginning stages, that they become the end rather than the means; and (3) to conceptualize a programme of study as step-by-step skill training.

Reimer (2/1989).

A study by Professor Justine Sergeant (McGill University, Toronto) involved recruiting ten healthy musicians who underwent brain scans while doing a series of keyboard and sight-reading tests. Unsurprisingly, the brain areas concerned with skilled movement of the fingers showed up during the scan, but the scan also indicated the existence of a neural network concerned exclusively with the appreciation of musical sounds. This area was activated when the pianists were listening to or playing music (in this case Bach's Partita BWV 767), but not when they were listening to or playing scales.

Wrathall (1992).

is what they have done. The instrumental teaching practices of Bartok, Mozart and Bach clearly show this principle at work. The invention of special studies should be part of the normal preparation for an instrumental teacher's lessons. Studies rarely lead naturally to the next area and main focus of the lesson, which is the chosen pieces. Both technical exercises and studies exist too often in self-fulfilling, watertight compartments unrelated to the main piece, which is where the main thrust of the student's attention lies.

The rehearsal of the main piece or pieces to be performed is normally done through the student playing, from notation, an agreed section. In many lessons this selection is made not by the teacher but by the student, so that any chance of the teacher linking prior learning of studies or technical exercises is lost. The lesson normally proceeds by the teacher observing the student's performance and occasionally commenting or stopping the performance to make a point of technique, skill or interpretation. This is done mainly through spoken instructions, but occasionally through deposing the student from the piano stool and demonstrating, or even leaning across them to play on the keyboard. The comments made by teacher to student tend to be observations and commands. If techniques of questioning are used at all, then closed questions are prevalent, mixed with instructions. "Do you see that passage there? Make certain that it is kept down. Place legato here more firmly. Do you understand?" Often instructions are given negatively – "Don't drop your wrist" – and concentrate mainly on what is going wrong in the performance.

These last observations move from the structure of the lesson to the practice of the teacher. Unlike the choir-trainer, modelling all the procedures and leading the way towards subtlety of musical expression by example and using music to convey music, the traditional piano teacher does not play, but acts rather as a critical audience. In too many instrumental lessons the only musical sounds heard are made by the students themselves, thereby providing only their own models for the development of their musical memories. Performance procedures are taught at second-hand through verbal descriptions and instructions, and there is rarely any challenge to the student to provide answers in any aspect of the playing. Aural acuity is stimulated only by accident; indeed the development of the musical memory and aural acuity are considered by many piano teachers to be part and parcel of quite another section of the student's musical course. Even in those situations where a piano teacher provides the only musical stimulus and input in a student's life, the development of the musical ear is left to holes and corners of the term, normally immediately before a formal examination has to be taken, and then it is rushed through as an obligation.

Many musicians lament what is known as the "vicious circle of bad practice" in instrumental teaching, which goes from higher education back into the early stages by the student copying the teacher and establishing the same poor practice in their own students. The lesson described above is to be found in many higher education institutions, including conservatoires, and these are the institutions most able to act as agents of change. The tendency to separate out technique from musical problem-solving is the most serious difficulty. As Simon Waters observes,

Instrumental teaching has significantly exacerbated this tendency, regarding technique as a relative fixity, separating instructed playing (from scores) from exploration of the possibilities of the instrument (improvisation/composition). Generations of music students have spent a significant proportion of their development as children and adults sitting in isolation fighting to assimilate an arbitrarily imposed technique. Ultimately this leads to a situation where (in an extreme characterisation) music students are socially unconfident and reliant on externally imposed incentives and timetables to work, whereas their visual arts equivalents have been allowed/given responsibility for many aspects of their own practice.

Waters (1994).

Putting the ear first as a basic principle

For example, let's take the case of two postgraduate teacher-training students learning first steps in acquiring kit-drumming skills. One student, of average academic ability but with a large amount of practical musical experience, can immediately make a circular movement on the side drum with a brush and tap out a complementary rhythm on the hi-hat while maintaining a syncopated beat on the bass-drum foot pedal, having had no previous drumming experience. She appears to be able to "relax into the feel of it". Yet a second student, of high academic standing and with considerable experience of organizing musical performances, deals with the same task by forcing himself to maintain what he knows he should do. The performance is stiff and tense and just manages to keep the ostinati together for a few repeats. The first student would appear to be able to engage her sensori-motor action through her right brain, feeling the shape of it rather than thinking it. The second student appears to have approached his task through the left brain. We all have experience of "thinking" doing and "feeling" doing.

A very common experience in all groups of instrumentalists is for them to be categorized into "sight-reader" or "player by ear". Within any group of music students there will be a majority who can sight-read well but who find great difficulty in memorizing and even more in "playing by ear". The minority who do play by ear and memorize easily are often also able to sight-read well. Sight-reading draws on the ability of the brain to scan and interpret music notation at a very fast speed. It also relies on the brain's ability to predetermine possibilities by estimating what is likely to arise. Such a task is made much more difficult when the amount of information to be taken in at once becomes excessive. Styles of music entirely new to the sight-reader make sight-reading more difficult.

The judgements which control the associative auditory functions that generate expectancies for harmonic progression in music are situated within the right brain. However, the judgements which interpret symbols for precise pitch and time are situated within the left brain. The more the sight-reader relies merely on "playing the notes", the more the player is engaging only the logical and analytical processes available in the left brain. Such playing of music is commonly paradoxically termed "unmusical". Indeed such an epithet is the

The most sublime labour of poetry is to give sense and passion to insensate things; and it is characteristic of children to take inanimate things in their hands and talk to them in play as if they were living persons ... This philological-philosophical axiom proves to us that in the world's childhood men were by nature sublime poets ...

Giambattista Vico, quoted in Chatwin (1987).

Play in its many forms (e.g. competition, chance, mimicry, vertigo) is one of the closest forms of performance activity to art making. The experiences of the two overlap substantially, yet such exploratory behaviour is undervalued and suppressed in most areas of human activity beyond childhood. Arts education offers one of the few possible avenues for acknowledging the significance of such behaviour.

Waters (1994).

strongest many examiners and judges use of a musical performance. In making use of such a paradox they are acknowledging that unless the brain integrates both hemispheres in different types of musical action the performance will suffer. Musical playing very likely means playing which uses both left and right brain in integration to generate fine judgements. Memorizing a piece of music considerably facilitates the performance, helping the whole brain to function efficiently.

"Playing" an instrument

It is significant that the word we use in many languages to describe the act of performance is "play". Playing is a life-skill, essential to our mental and physical development and well-being.

Children deprived of play opportunities suffer, and children beset by physical, mental or social deprivation show their distress through their play or lack of it. In play the child finds their own first connections between themselves and the outside world and learns to come to terms with it. Through play children learn to act as individuals separated from their parents, to become self-sufficient, to live with others, to make and break rules, to explore, create, destroy and build. Playing is a fundamental act of self-expression through which each individual grows and is a vital part of our learning process. Artistic action, it is argued by some writers, is a form of play substitute for the relationship between mother and child.

Play is essentially functionless, but has a pleasing effect. Through play a child seeks stimulus and uses up a good deal of energy in doing so. So far the parallel with musical playing holds true. Although our goal as players may well be the performance, and for professionals this means the real goal of earning money, in concrete terms musical playing has no quantifiable result. No one wins or loses. There is no final consummation and there is no threat or submission. Certainly musical performers use up a tremendous amount of energy and gain a great deal of pleasurable stimulus. The difference between a played action and a real one can be quite difficult to define. Specialists in play have suggested that the play of young children involves exaggerated, incompetent or awkward movement, as opposed to the real movements that cease to be play the moment they become effective. We use the term "play" across languages also to mean drama, and a "player" is an actor. It is perhaps here that we see adult "playing" most obviously in the exaggerated or awkward movement. However, few would claim that the movements made by performing musicians are, in terms of real-life tasks, competent or normal. In the sense that performing musicians use actions in their playing which in no manner relate to any parallels in real life, their actions can appear awkward or even incompetent in any other terms. The exaggerated diction or tone quality of an opera singer, without careful adjustment, would not produce competent or graceful speech in an everyday situation. Such performing can, indeed, be viewed as an adult form of play.

Play in children and adults involves special signals and codes. We play in order to find out something about ourselves and our relationships with others. In the play of young children there is a strong theme of relationships of children to adults, adults to adults and children to children. Certainly musical playing involves its own signals, codes and rules, and essentially performing is a shared act of communication. The vital element of communication is so often absent in otherwise competent performers, making a musical playing different from a musical performance. Communicating with the audience is difficult to define and doesn't often mean talking with them. In the best musical playing we can feel the communication between artist and listener through the actual sounds made and through the gestural content of the performance. Western performance practice often militates against effective use of communication skills, except in singers, who traditionally perform facing their audience. Too often instrumentalists are unaware of the importance of body language in communication and will seat themselves and dress themselves in a manner which does not enhance their performance. The more that performers rely on the recording as a means of communication, the less they may be aware of the need for relationships between people as a function of their playing.

Perhaps the most important aspect of play that one can observe in the activities of all young children is their obsession with making a sequence of actions and repeating them with a constant series of variations. Play is not set up through creative anarchy but starts with a defined set of rules which then are subjected to creative manipulation. Having started with the givens, the child will perform an almost endless sequence of versions of the same thing. The more creative the child is the more these variations will be subtle and personal, including an element of surprise. A child playing with a car in a sand-pit will accept most of the "givens" about cars and terrains, although they may happily break these rules when it suits them. Flying cars, for instance, are commonplace in such play behaviour.

In so many cultures other than our own, musical play also conforms exactly to this essential element of playing. The young sitarist will imitate the adult guru by endless repetitions and variations of musical sequences copied initially from the master musician; the shakuhachi player learns in this way, absorbing the theory of scales and ornament through imitative performance practice; the young Burundi drummer learns to drum by being part of the social group that drums and by joining in with the group as well as sitting by himself and, in the terms of sequentially variable action, playing for many hours. At the first WOMAD Festival in 1981, I had the task of interviewing the Burundi drummers for an educational television programme. I asked them to show me how they taught young drummers. The question disconcerted them. They did not understand the concept, since this was something they didn't do. After going into a huddle, they decided that they would put on a demonstration for me. The drummers formed a circle and placed their youngest group member in the centre. They drummed and he danced, and as he danced, one of the circle of drummers would reach out and cuff him or kick him severely, knocking him over. This was their conception of what Western music education must be like!

Within our culture this kind of behaviour can also be observed in the young kit-drummer and the folk fiddler. The youthful electric guitarist spends much time in repeating and varying well-known sequences or melodic motifs. In such performers we find creative improvising or even fully fledged composing as a normal behaviour deriving from good playing behaviour.

It is the "classically" trained performer yet again, however, who is told

Alan Jabbour, American folk fiddler and recording artist, in a lecture given in California in 1993 entitled "On the Trail of the Old-Time Fiddler", described how he, as a fully classically trained violinist, entered graduate school and became interested in research into folk fiddle playing. This involved him in working with traditional fiddle players in North Carolina. "Something else happened that I hadn't anticipated since my idea of being just a researcher wasn't something that they had in their head. All they could figure out was somebody who wanted to learn. So they encouraged me to bring my violin in and somehow or other, although I was shy and embarrassed, little by little, I began a long and laborious process of learning a new art. Sometimes I think that learning a new style of playing the violin is analogous to learning a new language. You know how to use vowels and consonants and to arrange things grammatically, and you might say it's the same with the fiddle, since you have the basics of your fingers and bow. What's worse is you have to learn a new way of learning. I had learned originally through rhythm annotation and the like, but suddenly thrust amongst the fiddlers themselves I was forced to strengthen my ear and to learn through the ear in a way that I never had to fully before. At first it was torture and I needed crutches. I tried annotating and looking at the annotations, but little by little I realized that I could learn a tune by ear, and the more I learned the easier it became. Now if I hear a tune that strikes me I can pick it up right away. … This new way of learning involves not tutelage by the master but active learning by the apprentice. The master plays, and it is the job of the apprentice to listen hard and to learn it as it goes by. The burden is on the apprentice to be an active learner."

never to "play by ear" and who is tied to the written page containing only the ideas of others from the very start. Without these essential improvised and repetitive elements of play, this kind of performing may never become "playing" in the true and full sense of the word. When musicians fully and trustingly learn to play with, on and though their instruments, they have the best chance to communicate with others through their music and they feel more at one both with their audience and with themselves. It is through this kind of play that the vital connection between body, intuition and logic that typifies good music practice is best made.

Quality learning

The newly set up Office of Standards in Education in England and Wales has produced a document of guidance for its inspectors that attempts to pin down in words the qualities of good learning. A primary definition is in the willingness of pupils to respond to challenges of tasks set by the teacher, to concentrate on them and to make good progress. This behaviour can readily be observed in most good instrumental teaching. However, the second definition is that learners must be able to adjust to working in different contexts, selecting appropriate methods and organizing effectively the resources they need. Here we encounter the first potential failure of traditional instrumental teaching, since it rarely encourages active learning, decision-making and selection of materials in pupils. The encouragement of a sense of enquiry implicit in the official description is mostly absent from any instrumental teaching. In this sense, much instrumental teaching does not qualify as teaching at all but only as training. The definition of good learning continues by describing a sense of enjoyment and commitment, and this is evident in current instrumental teaching practice, but it is followed by an emphasis on pupils who are sufficiently confident to raise questions and persevere with their work when answers are not available. The fact that, currently, Western music students of all ages are so heavily wedded to the weekly teaching session bears witness to the fact that they do not feel able to cope without the teacher. The asking of questions is rarely encouraged or stimulated in instrumental work, and the self-sufficiency implied in the official document on teaching quality is rarely found as an outcome. In fact the official document goes on to describe bad learning in terms of undue dependence on the teacher or uncritical use of resources, both common qualities of traditional instrumental teaching.

Finally the inspectors are asked to look for the ability of pupils to evaluate their own work and to come to realistic judgements about it, helping one another where appropriate. What is described is the encouragement of self-sufficiency in learning and in self-appraisal. Unsatisfactory learning is defined as that where children are unable to apply their learning to new contexts. Musicians who do learn these qualities through their instrumental lessons are likely to have been lucky enough to work with the very best teachers.

Resumé

●   The shared basic principles of instrumental teaching lie in the development of an individual musical response in students, giving them problem-solving skills which enable them to continue to learn and develop with positive self-criticism away from the teacher for the rest of their lives. At the heart of this development, alongside that of building strong psychomotor skills, is the establishment of an analytical and acute musical ear coupled with a creative approach to interpretation, reinterpretation and invention.

- The reading of notation is for many Western musicians a necessary skill, but overreliance on notation can be inimical to aural development and to a problem-solving approach to performing. We must also be open to the highly successful and centuries-old teaching and learning traditions of musicians of cultures all over the world.

- We must beware of the dangers of overencouraging sight-reading at the expense of more essential musical behaviours. This can lead to poor tone and intonation development.

- The cathedral musical tradition stems from Western European medieval practice and remains one of the few survivals of music education practice from our cultural past and, as such, provides us good ontological evidence for what works best in good practice. A chorister depends on an intensively working musical memory with notation acting as a memory aid. The combination of memory, aural alertness and gradually growing reading skills all based on the voice provides one of the most superb foundations for continuing musical practice. Because the essential skills are vocal, all the focus of attention is on the development of the ear and on the achievement of a particular kind of sound which goes with it.

- In instrumental teaching there is often a lack of learning focus and considered progression, either within the lesson or from lesson to lesson. The student is not encouraged to place new learning in context and to approach it from a whole-brain point of view. This separates out musical technique from problem-solving. The instrumental teacher acts only as a critical audience and not as a model, and students rarely hear any music-making that is not their own.

- We can learn to assimilate instrumental technique through either or both sides of the brain. Teachers should consider how well they truly encourage their pupils to play in the true sense of the word. One of the essentials of play is creative activity. Good learning is eventually defined by how well the pupil copes away from the teacher.

Teaching implications

Working with groups

Many instrumental teachers who work for large consortia in schools are forced into working with large groups by economics, but there are some who choose to do so. Example 1 is a typical lesson with one such teacher as a model for consideration for similar developments in other instrumental areas. The model is of a brass ensemble, not of the traditional brass-band type but a collection of brass players in a community, mixing brass-band instruments and orchestral brass. Unlike so much ensemble work, a great deal of the lesson is spent by the performers looking directly at the conductor and taking cues from her. Their musical memories are expanded and the interaction between body and mind is sharpened, particularly enhancing right-brain procedures, but providing stimulus for left-brain thinking through chord structures and scale patterns, syncopations, etc. Soloists are encouraged and there is a general feeling of empowerment as well as of achievement in performance in the usual sense.

Example 1: Rehearsal of one hour with junior band containing children from nine upwards, both male and female, and parents

Lesson focus: Confidence in improvisation and extending musical memory and aural acuity
Materials: Appropriate instrumental parts for three pieces for band

The conductor/teacher begins the rehearsal without any formal announcement by playing a short rhythmic two-pitch phrase on her cornet which the band is expected to echo. The whole band, used to this procedure, imitates her and a sequence of exercises follows, each example taxing the players a little more in pitch and rhythm, including minor versions of major intervals and exploring arpeggios. There is a good deal of joking with various groups, such as trombones, when the phrases get quicker and more agile. Inexperienced players are assisted by exaggerated miming of the valve finger patterns during their echo.

The teacher then proceeds to "dictate" aurally simple rounds in the same manner, line by line. She chooses "Three Blind Mice" first and divides the band into three for them to play it as a round. "Row, Row" in the same manner is followed by "Frère Jacques". Ultimately the band is encouraged to play all of these as rounds together, making three partnership songs. The next activity is a question and answer extension of the first activity. Answerers are first chosen by the teacher pointing to them just as she ends her question phrase. Players are encouraged to stand up to play their answers. A basic repeated riff is "dictated" to all the band, and volunteers are commissioned to stand up and improvise over the riff. A 12-bar blues structure is then suggested, and the band first plays the root of the chords as the teacher beats time and shows the chord number (1, IV or V) by holding up fingers. As they continue to do this the teacher herself improvises over the roots of the chords. The band is then asked to add the other notes of the arpeggio while some volunteers play extended improvisations. Finally sevenths are also added while the teacher and more confident players improvise.

The band is then asked to turn to the copies of a piece they have rehearsed several times. Having played it through once they are asked to sing through the whole piece, each player singing his or her part. Next they are asked to play it with their copies reversed on their stands. Posture is constantly corrected in a positive manner. At one point the teacher puts out all the lights and the band continues to play until she puts them on again, just before the finish of the piece. Lastly they play with the copy, and the performance is tightened up through critical analysis by the conductor.

During the rehearsal of two more pieces, young band members are asked to volunteer to conduct in the teacher's place. She stands behind the volunteer and helps them with their stick control. The last volunteer conductor is asked to imitate "Mr Bean", which means that they can slow down, pause or quicken up at will and the band must follow them in every detail. A final play-through of a piece they know well concludes the rehearsal.

(*From Frances Taylor, Conductor, Clevedon, Junior Community Band, Avon*)

By joining together the end of one individual lesson and the beginning of another, in Example 2 the teacher achieves interaction between pupils and also saves herself a lot of repetition. All the techniques described could apply to an individual lesson as well, but the teacher here makes group work a positive advantage to both sides. She extends the musical memory and aural acuity of her pupils by approaching first through right-brain techniques based on melody and prediction and then introduces increasingly more logical left-brain thinking through transposition and theory of harmony.

Example 2: A ten-minute group piano lesson with two pupils

Lesson focus: Learning to improvise melodies and harmony
Materials: Two pianos

A piano lesson with two eight-year-old pupils uses ten minutes at the end of Child A's lesson and the beginning of Child B's lesson in group teaching of formal improvisation processes. There are two pianos in the studio. Both children have Grade III ABRSM examinations. The session starts with both children at the same piano, standing at the keyboard, with the teacher at the other. The teacher plays middle C and asks Child A to find the same pitch on their keyboard. Child B is asked to play C an octave above and the teacher explains that her melodies will lie within that range.

First the teacher improvises a series of short formal melodies leading obviously to the tonic but stopping short of it. The children, in turn, play the implied pitch. In the next exercise the teacher plays half a melody, explaining that she wants the pupil to finish it and that it will finish on the tonic – again in C. This is successfully done several times by both children and the teacher asks Child B to choose a change of key: he chooses G and the teacher makes a quick revision of the map of the scale, reminding him of F sharp. Further standard half-melody patterns are improvised by the teacher, each ending in an imperfect cadence, the children's replies always ending on a perfect.

Now the exercise is split between both children at the same keyboard. Child A begins a melody in the same manner as the teacher, Child B closes it, and vice versa. They exchange places to do this. The two key centres used so far are both explored at the suggestion of the teacher. The teacher prompts, comments and reinforces by playing at her own piano.

The lesson moves on to asking one child to improvise the whole melody in C while the other child explores, adding an appropriate bass. A certain amount of trial and error occurs with prompting by the teacher from her keyboard of the "How about trying this?" type. The exercise is repeated several times, challenging Child A to remember exactly what they played and Child B to find the pattern of the bass notes implied. The teacher suggests adding arpeggios in the bass and Child B explores the idea. The exercise is then repeated with the children reversing roles.

Finally the teacher moves Child A to her piano and stands with Child B, who is now working out bass and vamped chord using both hands to Child A's melody. Child A plays their melody in octaves. Child B manages to find each of the three primary triads and to fit them appropriately to the melody, with a little hesitation. To finish, the teacher asks them to choose a different key and to repeat the exercise, which they find that they can do well a second time after one hesitant attempt.

(*From Vera Crawford-Smith: Nailsea ISM, 1992*)

Example 3, from Key Stage 3, provides an excellent example of the integration of performing and composing as a single process. It also shows how interaction between teacher and pupil, and between pupil and pupil, can enhance the lesson and stimulate a problem-solving attitude without sacrificing any of the traditional technical focus. Note particularly how the playing of scales and studies has become the essence of the lesson and is fully integrated into a musical approach through the study. Pupils taught technical exercises in this way have a good chance of being able to enagage their whole musical brain in the playing of exercises, making them essentially musical in effect and providing a musical rationale for this work. This should ensure a better rate of transference of learning from technical exercise to application in practice. I am completely endebted to Chris Morgan and his Instrumental Services team in Cornwall for the next two examples.

Example 3: Woodwind lesson at Key Stage 3 with two clarinet pupils in a shared lesson

Lesson Focus: To increase articulation, knowledge of scale/mode and improvisation skills
Materials: Demnitz Study in A minor, Adagio (see Appendix)

Before the teacher asks both pupils to play the A minor melodic scale together she suggests that it is done very slowly. She asks the pupils to decide what tempo and dynamic marking they might start with, and how it should progress. After they have performed, the teacher discusses refinements of their performance with the pupils, asking them what adjustments they might suggest, for instance in intonation, and how they might achieve this.

Next, using the same tempo, one pupil repeats each note four times (soft tonguing, mezzo staccato) while the other pupil goes at half speed. After the performance, dynamics are discussed and attention is focused on intonation to consider whether it has improved, and they repeat the task.

Question and answer exercises follow, first initiated by the teacher then passed on to the pupils, each to take the role of questioner and answerer in turn. A minor melodic scale is still used, first in the low register, then in the upper register, then crossing the break.

The pupils turn to the Demnitz study in their books and they are asked to explain the intentions behind the study and what its musical features are. Each pupil performs the study and they both are asked what they noticed about the performance. How did they come to the choice of tempo and what mood did they hope to convey? What is the purpose of the accents and how they should be articulated? What kind of finger movement ensures a smooth legato? How will they articulate bar 8? What effect is created if they leave out the slurs in bars 1 and 2? What effect is created by shortening or lengthening the crotchet in bar 2?

As a last activity the teacher asks both pupils to perform the study in the form of a "solo and chorus". She asks them to examine the structure of the study and to decide where the appropriate points are at which each player might hand over to the other or come together.

Finally work is set for next week. The pupils are both asked to compose an "adagio" in the aeolian mode. They should consider which feature/features and style to explore and to build into it those elements of their playing that they feel work best. The teacher comments on one good aspect of one pupil's technique and a different one for the other, stimulating different responses from them. The teacher suggests that the form should be solo and chorus. They are also asked to practise the Demnitz study to perform for next week, aiming for greater dynamic contrast, smoother legato, etc.

(from Performing Arts Cornwall, Director Chris Morgan, 1994)

Example 4: Individual string lesson at Key Stage 4

Lesson focus: Working towards a performance of Elgar's *Chanson de Nuit*, op.15, no. 1 (see Appendix)

(Note: This lesson depends a great deal upon the discussion being two-way. Too many instrumental teachers consider that they "discuss" things when they actually do no more than dictate to the student.)

Warming up for the lesson begins with scales. The teacher emphasizes the special focus of listening for and improving the quality of tone (especially sul.G) and finger-strengthening. One octave and a fifth of G major (the key of the piece) is played in half-notes. A starting dynamic is discussed and the first time any fingering is used, the second time only one finger, the third the first finger, and so on.

The teacher turns next to an exploration of vibrato by playing a passage from the piece with both slow and quick vibrato. A discussion follows about appropriateness of both types and when one might move from one to the other.

Next an exercise is given to test bow speed and pressure. An open D is played by the pupil, making the whole bow last for eight beats, then six, then four, then two. The teacher provides an accompaniment through improvising on his own violin. They discuss how the quality of sound can be maintained throughout.

Next they turn to the Elgar, first considering and discussing the title and intention of the piece and listening to an extract on tape of the orchestral version. In the play-through the teacher accompanies at the piano, and after they concentrate more closely on the relationship with the accompaniment and the accompanist. Many questions occur, such as, "What are you considering when choosing your opening dynamic? What do you need to take special care about in bar 13? How will you come in together? What's the bass line doing in bars 2 and 3? What does this chord progression in bars 2 and 3 suggest?" The first four bars are played and gradations of dynamic are considered. "Why does this matter?" asks the teacher.

The next series of questions include, "During the first 12 bars, where are there small counter-motifs in the accompaniment?" (bars 6 and 8). "Can you sing or play them? What are the musical implications for you? What happens in the accompaniment at bar 17? How does it compare with the previous section? What is the effect?"

The teacher observes that he cannot hear the sixteenth-note in the phrase in bars 17 and 18 in the pupil's performance. He suggests that he will try to demonstrate what he is hearing and asks the pupil what the effect is. The pupil imitates the poor example and then the good one several times. Pupil and teacher discuss how both accompanist and soloist can coordinate in bars 17 and 18 and if the piano should also respond to the diminuendi in the same manner.

In bars 26 to 28 they discuss the change of texture and how it is created. The teacher asks the pupil to suggest how the feeling of conversation between solo and accompaniment can be enhanced.

Before a final play-through, the teacher requests that the pupil become more familiar with the accompaniment during the week, and practise playing the bass and top lines of the accompaniment while thinking about or singing their own part in relation to the accompaniment, where they can best lead and how they can achieve it.

(*From Performing Arts Cornwall, Director Chris Morgan, 1994*)

Notions of good practice in instrumental teaching

The first part of establishing good practice must derive from teachers considering carefully what the ideal outcome of their instrumental teaching should be. It is too easy to fall into the trap of self-perpetuation. If teachers are to become models of good practice for their students, then they must carefully review their own attitudes and practices and, with each student, establish early on what the student's aspiration is. Setting targets and goals each term based on these aspirations as well as on the teachers' own or even external examination imperatives is essential. These goals must be recorded and constantly referred to. Repertoire given to a student must take into account what a student personally wishes to achieve. Being aware of the many dangers of teaching towards artificial goals is one of the greatest insights teachers can have into their own practice. Examinations are, even at degree level, a means to an end, and not ultimate goals themselves. If, however, the student's aspirations and the examination's demands coalesce, and often they do, then all is well.

The second part is to ensure that musical sound is involved in the greatest part of the lesson. In the early stages of learning this will mean that the teacher must play more than the student, but even in the later stages, the sound of what the teacher requires from the student should come as much from the teacher as from the student. After all, when students are away from their teacher they have nothing but their aural memories of what is good about tone colour, intonation and articulation to guide them. Building up sound memories is an essential part of a teacher's job.

The third part is to establish the best physical habits of posture and technique. Posture has to be learnt and practised as hard as technical exercises, and the teacher must find a positive attitude to encourage a feeling of intimacy between body and instrument in the student so that playing becomes second nature. Teachers must be absolutely up to date with their information of possible medical problems associated with their instrument and remain always alert for signs of these occurring.

The fourth part is to establish a balance between the demands of sight-reading from notation and developing an aural memory. Committing musical procedures to the long-term memory is an essential part of this process, as is learning to improvise and to build up an understanding of how music works through established traditional patterns of scales, harmonies, etc.

The fifth part is to make the exploration of musical repertoire a journey of discovery for students that will continue for the rest of their life. More advanced students should be taught how to make mind-maps of those pieces on which they will be spending a good deal of their time, by making diagrams of the piece. These can include any factual information, interpretative ideas, editing points, details of technical problems, impressions of the feelings given by the music and something of the meaning of the piece. Students should keep practice diaries and music common-place books which record their personal musical development.

Lastly the teacher should establish effective record-keeping and assessment procedures that take into account goals set and achieved, records of summative examinations and formative records kept by both teacher and student, and parent's comments and observations.

Guidelines for good practice

Structuring the lesson

Each lesson must be individually planned. Each element of the lesson plan should clearly show progression and interlinking of learning between technical exercises, improvisation and performance of works. The teacher should be "in the driving seat" and should have a clear programme to ensure progression. At the same time there must be the possibility of flexibility when the occasion demands.

Working with individuals and small and large groups

Lessons given to groups of three or more should be planned as a group experience with material adapted for its constituent members. Learning speeds and varying skill levels should be accounted for in flexible musical arrangements, featuring accompaniments and solos. Where feasible, students should be engaged in playing for most of the lesson. This will depend on the instrument's characteristics and the students' stamina; young brass students, for instance, have little staying power at first. Individual or paired lessons should likewise be planned as such, taking into account the needs of the students. Adapted or created materials should allow maximum musical engagement. The greatest part of the musical information should come directly from the teacher's example. Teachers should never forget the privilege many of them have in working with individuals and the ease of communication this provides them in contrast with the classroom teacher. It is too easy to forget and to take this privilege for granted.

Teachers working with large groups in the early stages have particular problems but must never forget the model of the choir-trainer. It is possible to involve large groups of beginners in a real musical experience, and this must be the goal of the teacher. If this is achieved then all other problems of differentiation and skill fall into place.

Modelling sound

It is from the teacher's own example as a musician that students learn best. Tone quality, phrasing, dynamic and articulation should all be part and parcel of the earliest lessons. Teachers should encourage their students' listening skills by placing themselves away from the pupil enough so that the signal is picked up by the ear and not the eye. Good posture is, of course, modelled visually. Information should be given through musical cues whenever possible and the pupil's aural acuity challenged and developed in this way. The teacher's own singing voice is an essential in this area of conveying accurate musical information, and the correct singing and naming of intervals should be second nature.

Use of language and communication and interaction skills

An ideal lesson would be one in which the teacher conveyed all the musical information musically, but this is unlikely to be possible. Teachers should use heuristic methods of questioning, mixing open and closed questions appropriately and drawing information out of their students rather than pushing it in. They should encourage a problem-solving attitude in technical problems and in matters of interpretation by asking questions and following through the answers with more questions. Students should be encouraged to explore alternative strategies. They should also be encouraged to play from memory a great deal, particularly the pieces they like to play best. Teachers must be prepared to question students on what they do and to follow the answers through with a respect for the students' opinions. A positive attitude is vital.

Teachers should be aware of the need to use musical technical language in the correct context, particularly concentrating on naming structural, intervallic and harmonic procedures by their appropriate terminology.

Technical exercises and their uses and abuses

Technique must be built up through appropriate technical exercises. Such exercises should always be placed in a real musical context by example from written works or by specially invented examples. Students should play technical exercises and studies with expression. They should be encouraged to work out basic fingering patterns and scalic shapes for themselves from first principles.

Planning and creating materials

Both the teacher and the pupil should generate musical exercises to extend technique. Improvisation should be a standard part of the lesson and the improvisation by teacher and pupil of exercises to address a particular technical problem should be a regular feature.

Problem-solving as a central issue

Teachers must strive to avoid the teacher-directed didactic approach, especially in an individual lesson, when a heuristic approach can be maximized. Information can always be expressed as a syllogism or basic problem which the pupil must solve.

Listening to the students and serving their needs

Instrumental teachers are renowned for making good individual relationships with their students but not always for finding out what it is that the pupil actually aspires to and wants to get from their lessons. Instrumental teachers should see themselves as educators and facilitators and not merely as trainers.

Encouraging listening and appraising

Students should be encouraged to find out as much as possible about the music they are playing. This can be done through worksheets and library research, and the creation of mind-maps on special set pieces should be encouraged. Appraisal of the music should be an essential part of the discussion of the lesson.

Using the voice

Instrumental lessons as well as vocal lessons should encourage the use of the student's voice to express essential musical ideas of expression. This will best be encouraged by the model provided by the teacher. Singing along as you play encourages an internalizing of the line.

Techniques of assessment, monitoring and recording progress

Both teacher and student should keep some account of the lesson in writing. The teacher needs to develop a shorthand system which records progress and achievement, keeping onerous recording to a minimum. It should be done "on the job" and not left to weekends or evenings, or even worse to the end of terms. The student should keep a diary of their practice and of their discovery of music and of themselves. In their practice diary they should be encouraged to note what they find most difficult technically and to explain what they have done to tackle this. They should also be encouraged to keep a music common-place book in which they record anything new in writing that comes to them as thoughts and ideas, as quotations, as prose and as poetry. Common-place books should be pleasing to handle – good paper and cover – and, as well as writing, can contain musical notation, drawings, paintings and even mind-maps. Practice diaries and common-place books should form part of summative assessments which will be an amalgam of the teacher's records and the student's records plus any appropriate external examination. An important issue is not to allow the latter to become the only form of assessment, since formal instrumental examinations test only one area and one kind of performing. At the beginning of each term, teacher and pupil should discuss aspiration and, by negotiation, set agreed goals. Formative assessment should be based on the amount of achievement of these.

Motivating practice

Students need to practise regularly and with ease. They must learn the habits of good practice technique from the teacher through modelling in the lesson: they must be shown how to practise. Essentially, students must practise postural relaxation, and this must be formalized into a procedure taught and demonstrated by the teacher. This must include dealing with stress and being aware of the physical dangers of instrumental performing. Students must be encouraged to practise as much from memory as from notation, when good posture and a relaxed body, rather than the distant music stand with the dots and lines and awkward page turns, can be the central focus of attention. They must be given clear tasks and guidelines in each lesson and these must be recorded by both student and teacher.

Using tapes

The most certain way of documenting progress is actually to record the lesson each time. The pupils can take tapes with them and use them to play against, to listen to and to remind themselves what their tasks are. Tapes should include accompaniments prepared by the teacher, either as recordings of piano/keyboards or by using backing-track tapes made using sequencers and multi-track recording facility. Tapes emphasize the sound of the lesson and help the student to ensure that the notation from which they constantly work will become for them a sounding symbol.

SOUNDING THE SYMBOL

In this short final chapter I will draw together the basic principles upon which I consider good practice in music education to be based and set them out under the four categories of teaching most prevalent in British education. The first category is the class-based generalist teacher in primary education who I will assume has little or no music training and background, but is both willing and motivated to attempt music education with the class. The second is that of the specialist trained teacher who works in the classroom, mostly with secondary age children but in some areas and individual schools across the whole school age-range. The third category is the instrumental teacher working alongside the school or higher education system. The fourth is the specialist teacher in tertiary, higher or adult education.

"Sounding the symbol" describes the way in which good teaching can ensure that whatever symbol system we use to record music triggers the correct sounds in our head. In describing achievement by the age of seven in music education, the latest government consultation document suggests that pupils must "relate symbols to sounds and sounds to symbols". Although I would have put the "sound" before the "symbol" for its symbolic value, this learning target addresses one of the crucial areas of expertise associated with Western musical tradition.

Getting notation into perspective

Standard musical notation is not only here to stay, it has profoundly affected the development and aspiration of music and musicians. Chord notation and tablature that shows instrumental fingering are both in common use and Sol-fa is a very helpful teaching and learning device. All these symbol systems need to be experienced by children when they are appropriate to learning, but all of them carry with them an inherent and fundamental learning problem. Because written symbols are processed largely by the left brain it is possible and likely that, since we are all so much more adept at left-brain work, the right brain can be by-passed, the necessary body action being triggered solely by the left brain. A musical action can result that may be profoundly unmusical in quality simply because the fine processing system for sound in the brain has been circumnavigated.

Musical memory and learning

Good practice, at all those teaching levels I have identified, must work to promote the development of the musical memory, advantaging the right brain wherever possible and ensuring that the connection through to the left brain is lively. The habitual musical connection across the corpus callosum will be fundamentally from right to left (and then back and forth) if the early training of the musical brain has been well

There is evidence for right hemispheral specialization for musical functions. Experts, however, showed greater disruption with the right hand. This supports the hypothesis of a leftward shift of hemispheric specialization for the performance of musical tasks after academic musical training.

Fabbro, F. et al. (1990). "Opposite musical-manual interference in young vs expert musicians", Neuropsychologia, 28.

Just as technology has often limited man's personal capacities, so it can also extend them. Technology itself is neutral and can be employed to make man more or less human. It has to be refocused towards an extension of our personal capacities rather than a diminution of them.

Ornstein, R. E. (1977). The Psychology of Consciousness. 2nd edn, New York: Harcourt Brace.

founded. The goal is to achieve a full balance of right- and left-brain operation plus the ability to move completely into one area or the other at will when the operation and circumstances demand.

The issues of differentiation, equal opportunities and special needs will be assumed as basic to all good teaching strategy and not referred to separately here. In planning the music curriculum at all levels we should be guided by the ontological principle, particularly at the beginning stages of any skill or technique. From our knowledge of the past we can inform our present. It can help us look for key learning experiences and to order learning for others. New skills and techniques can be learnt at any age, not least in higher and continuing education, and there will always be a need for teachers to consider the spiral nature of learning. Revisiting old things in new ways and, if necessary, becoming child-like again in attitude while laying new learning foundations are essentials for good learning in all areas, none more so than music. The best teachers are those who are themselves perpetual learners.

Teachers without specialist training must be prepared to learn with and through their pupils. It will be important for them, or their schools, to invest in the best available support materials to provide them with programmes of singing and listening repertoire and ideas for composing and performing. The most vital equipment is good playback machinery. With good support materials available, an open mind and a positive attitude towards the subject are the main prerequisites.

Using micro-technology

Computers are readily available in the infant classroom, but there is not a great deal of suitable software presently available in music education for this age-group. Some of the best programmes so far are those which allow the pupil to select melodic modules and join them together to produce a melodic shape. The problem built in to most programmes, however, is that they do not give much aid to aural awareness. In placing visual perception and choice first they tend to engage a left-brain reaction in children, approaching the act of composing, as it were, from the wrong brain side. Programmes originally designed for special education also have a great deal to offer in the development of interaction between the child and the computer through using light pens, and through touching the screen to make sound. Programmes which enhance the synthesis between shape, texture, colour, line and their sound equivalents offer a great potential for right-brain stimulus, and new "paint" programmes are being created where each "brush-stroke" produces its sound equivalent. This kind of interaction between the young child and computer to create music holds a great deal of potential, particularly with the use of CD-ROMs, but neither the hard- nor the software necessary for such programmes to operate effectively is yet easily available to the average infants' classroom.

For older children the most advantageous developments have been those of linked music keyboards and sequencers. These can be found at present in various formats, either as separate music keyboards with built-in sequencers or as computer software programmes offering an on-screen equivalent to the keyboard. Keyboards can also be linked through MIDI to computer programmes, and this combination offers the most powerful tool which can be operated by children of seven, eight and over and carry right through to professional studio practice. Electronic keyboards on their own, used as instruments in their own right, have a good deal to offer in the classroom but have certain inherent dangers of which teachers need to be well aware. The issues are:

a) developing a playing technique. Keyboards need to be learnt as instruments like any others. Children can use the "one-finger" approach, as many of us do when typing, but what they can do will be very limited, as many of us find as typists.

b) key size tends to be very small on any but the more expensive instruments, making good playing difficult.

c) the built-in amplification is weak, thus causing the actual sound the keyboard makes to be less useful for ensemble work. Linking the instrument up to separate amplifiers cures this problem but provides other resource problems and complicates the physical environment with extra controls and leads.

d) the built-in sounds provided on many machines are limited and leave much to be desired aesthetically.

e) using keyboards with headphones can supply a quick answer to intrusive sound in the classroom but can also provide difficult problems of monitoring for the teacher and isolation for the pupil.

f) manufacturers appear unwilling to provide machines in which both the rhythm section and the demonstration programmes can be either isolated or made immobile. Both these things provide teachers with unwanted and unnecessary challenges to good class discipline.

Sequencing programmes provide the ability to create music through improvisation and composition either on-screen or through using a keyboard. Some programmes provide alternative on-screen clones of guitars so that guitarists can "finger" the screen diagram using the mouse. Melodic and harmonic lines can be multi-tracked, layered one upon the other, providing the texture required. Material can be processed through input by playing in real time (like a proper performance) or in step-time (where each step of a performance is put into the computer separately without any reference to real time). Material can also be transposed, speeded up or slowed down through manipulating the programme. Some sequencing packages interact with notation programmes, allowing the composer or improviser immediately to view their work in standard notation and for this to be printed out. Instrumental parts can also be accessed and printed out from a full score. Notation programmes that will play through what has been written, although complicated and expensive, offer much to young composers, allowing them instantly to hear their music, however complex. Once the software user techniques have been mastered, much of the drudgery of writing and copying is removed.

Musical training programmes are few and far between and tend to be based on rather mechanical theorizing through notation. There are one or two very good aurally based analytical programmes that will promote and test aural awareness. These can include melodic dictation and chordal analysis. There are still problems of learning transference and programmes are still in an early stage of development. A great virtue of such programmes is the privacy they afford the pupil, and the detailed account of the learning process it provides the teacher without involving them in repetitive tutorial sessions.

The CD-ROM offers the greatest possibilities for good learning, and these have already been described in Chapter 6.

A most vital technical skill for specialists and instrumental teachers is in the use and developing application of such music-devoted micro-technology, either using sequencers built into keyboards or on computer software. Improvising, composing, arranging and recording and mixing down multi-tracked accompaniments is now one of the staple features of a music specialist's "tool-kit". This work can be enhanced considerably if the user has keyboard facility, but, using step-time, musicians who play any instrument can adapt their skills and knowledge to operating the electronic keyboard. Such a facility allows exploration of a much wider range of performance material both in and out of the classroom than was available in the past. Backing tracks can be mixed in with live voices and also with live instrumental work to stiffen, enhance and provide instrumental lines and effects otherwise unavailable. We are only at the beginning of such developments, and no doubt this account will be hopelessly out of date even before it is published.

Breadth of musical experience

Graduates of colleges and universities should normally be conversant with the basics of musicology, but many will find themselves proficient and knowledgeable only in a relatively small area of Western European musical history. Recently some higher education courses have been expanding to allow for students to gain some experience in other cultural traditions. Any music specialist now must be at least conversant with the music and traditions of the main world blocks of musical culture of India, Africa, Indonesia, China and Japan as well as the folk music of Europe and the Americas.

Alongside this sympathy with and understanding of the vernacular and high art music of other countries goes a need to be sympathetic and conversant with the musical vernacular and subcultures of our own society. Specialists, and those working in tertiary and higher education, have to cultivate a wide and all-inclusive musical taste coupled with practical experience in many musical structures and techniques. This could mean being able to improvise over a figured bass, on a chorale melody, using Japanese shakuhachi scales or blues chord sequences, or over a rock and roll or salsa riff; it could mean constructing an African or South American drumming sequence in step-time on a drum machine, playing a basic disco beat on a drum kit or an Indian tala on tabla, singing using Balkan vocal techniques, or performing in early Baroque style. Above all the music specialist teacher must be able to make the sounds of music leap from the page for their pupils, either from musical notations including tablature and chord symbols or from written analyses of masterworks. There is no subject area where a dedication to and love of the subject is more important to a specialist's success. When music learning has been most successful there is a fluent and effortless interaction between thinking, feeling and doing, and the sound and the symbol coalesce.

The basic principles of good practice

The generalist teacher

For infants and children under the age of seven, the class-based teacher should:

- plan a mixture of ten-minute "drip-feed" activities for short daily input alongside longer weekly lessons.

For juniors, they need to:

- plan for and balance group and individual work in performing and composing in classes from the age of seven onwards by ensuring space and opportunity as well as resources and learning focus, integrated with weekly teacher-directed lessons.

For all age-groups, they should:

- encourage the development of musical memory reinforced by movement, and help children to become inquisitive about the structures of music
- make singing with the teacher a core activity
- provide individual listening opportunities and the appropriate resources, and regular class listening experiences linking story and music and encouraging cross-curriculum work
- plan music in assembly, both performing and listening, assuring a wide experience of all types of music and involving pupils in presentation
- collect evidence of progress and development from individual and paired work
- help children to invent their own notations for sounds they create and hear, and introduce elements of standard notations through flash cards and scan-reading
- use micro-technology to enhance music learning
- encourage the practice of music in children both in and outside school through positive attitudes, making sure that pupils' musical experience outside school is kept on record in the school.

The specialist teacher

As well as the foregoing, the specialist teacher should:

- promote detailed aural analysis through the progressive development of musical memory, using movement as reinforcement to learning
- use personal musical performing skills to provide models of good practice and pass on these skills to children
- improvise and compose for and with pupils, and provide both open and closed improvising and composing projects
- provide every opportunity for composers to hear their compositions in the best performances available
- encourage children to scan-read notation as they sing and to learn to sing from notation once they have a good enough memory base of the style; help children to scan-read notation to a high level as they listen and to perform instrumentally from notation once the playing of their instrument is natural and comfortable

- encourage a sense of enquiry into the structures and techniques from which music is constructed, starting with focused listening and moving into analytical thinking
- promote high-level performing opportunities both in and out of the classroom, ensuring an educationally sound connection between the two
- promote the use of micro-technology in music, especially CD-ROMs, sequencing and notating programmes
- collect evidence of progress and development from individual and paired work.

The instrumental teacher

The instrumental teacher should:

- promote detailed aural analysis through progressive development of musical memory
- use their performing skills to provide models of good practice and pass on these skills to children
- found and promote the best, most musically effective and most health-promoting postural and physical movement and control
- improvise and compose for and with their pupils, and provide stimulus for pupils' improvising and composing projects
- plan lessons for individuals thematically, inventing new materials appropriate to the pupil's interest and need and ensuring that all elements of the lesson interact appropriately and are progressive
- promote discussion, enquiry, independent learning and discovery
- collect evidence of progress and development from individual work
- help pupils to perform instrumentally from notation once the playing of their instrument is natural and comfortable
- promote high-level performing opportunities
- use micro-technology to allow students to assess their performance and review their lessons and as support in accompaniments and ensemble work.

The teacher in higher education

The specialist in tertiary and higher education should:

- promote a sense of enquiry, discussion, exploration and self-determination in students
- promote detailed aural analysis through the progressive development of musical memory
- promote programmes that continue emphasis upon the basic skills of performing and composing while challenging students to listen widely and in great detail, with no stylistic barriers, either subcultural or cross-cultural
- promote detailed analysis and discussion of compositional techniques of a variety of styles and cultural derivations, emphasizing aural perception
- promote an awareness of historical development across cultures through aurally based analysis and exploration, including performance, backed up with appropriate reading
- promote the exploration of cross-curricular connections with music, especially but not exclusively in other arts

- provide every opportunity for composers to hear their compositions in the best performances available
- promote high-level performing opportunities both in and out of the classroom, ensuring an educationally sound connection between the two
- provide the highest quality live performances for student audiences
- promote the use of micro-technology in music, especially CD-ROMs, sequencing and notating programmes.

Coda

To assist and develop musical memory and perception, and in order to speculate and to preserve music, we need to use written notational symbol systems, but these systems are of secondary importance to the sounds they symbolize. Ultimately, musical meaning can be expressed, approached and understood only through its medium of sound. No mark on paper, no word or symbol, written or spoken, can in any way convey to someone who has never heard it what music is and what it represents for us. Music is a sounding symbol. The bottom line is that the successful study of music depends on developing the ear. Nothing is more important than this.

Appendix

Divali Song (page 48)
Words and Music by George Odam

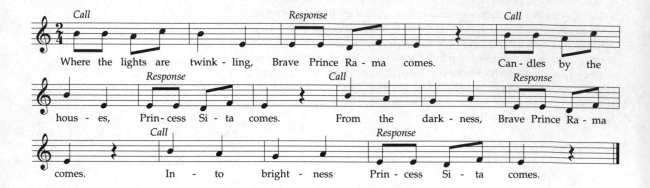

Call Where the lights are twink-ling, *Response* Brave Prince Ra-ma comes. *Call* Can-dles by the hous-es, *Response* Prin-cess Si-ta comes. *Call* From the dark-ness, Brave Prince Ra-ma comes. *Call* In-to bright-ness *Response* Prin-cess Si-ta comes.

I don't mind (Part I) (page 50)
Words and Music by David Eddleman

Melody 1 I don't mind if you sing;— I don't mind if you dance; I don't mind as long as you don't mind if I should sing, too, just by chance.

Melody 2 You'll nev-er go wrong keep-ing a song sing-ing a-long. You'll see you've got to be hap-py and free sing-ing a mel-o-dy.

I Don't Mind *Refrain*

John Barleycorn (page 51)

English folk song

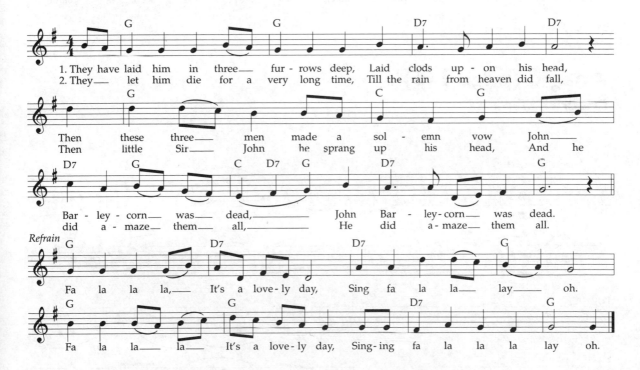

3. And they let him stand till the midsummer day,   And so became a man,
   Till he looked both pale and wan,   And so become a man.
   Then little Sir John he grew a long beard,   *Refrain*

If I Were You (page 51)
Words by Connie Rybak   Music by Lawrence Eisman

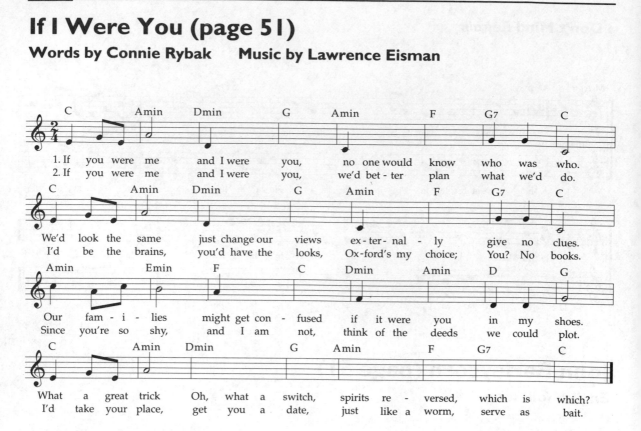

1. If you were me and I were you, no one would know who was who.
2. If you were me and I were you, we'd bet - ter plan what we'd do.

We'd look the same just change our views, ex - ter - nal - ly give no clues.
I'd be the brains, you'd have the looks, Ox-ford's my choice; You? No books.

Our fam - i - lies might get con - fused if it were you in my shoes.
Since you're so shy, and I am not, think of the deeds we could plot.

What a great trick Oh, what a switch, spirits re - versed, which is which?
I'd take your place, get you a date, just like a worm, serve as bait.

© Connie Rybak

Adagio (page 116)
Friedrich Demnitz

Chanson de nuit (page 117)

Edward Elgar

Bibliography

Aitkin, L. (1986). *The Auditory Midbrain*. Totowa, NJ: Humana Press.

Austin, D. (1994). "Neighbours theme learned in the womb", *The Independent*. May.

Balzano, G. J. (1986). "What are musical pitch and timbre?" *Music Perception*, 3, 3.

Bloom, B. F. (1956, 1964). *Taxonomy of Educational Objectives: a Classification of Educational Goals*, 2 vols. London: Longman.

Blacking, J. (1987). *A Common-Sense View of All Music*. Cambridge: Cambridge University Press.

Bogen, J. E. (1969). "The other side of the brain", *Bulletin of the Los Angeles Neurological Societies*, 34, 2.

Buzan, T. and B. (1989). *The Mind Map Book*. London: BBC Publications.

Chatwin, B. (1987). *The Songlines*. London: Picador.

Cole, H. (1974). *Sounds and Signs*. Oxford: Oxford University Press.

Coleman, S. N. (1992). *Creative Music for Children*. New York: Putnam.

Cooke, D. (1962). *The Language of Music*. London: Oxford University Press.

Cutting, J. E. and Rosner, B. S. (1974). "Categories and boundaries in speech and music", *Perception and Psychophysics*, 16, 3.

Department of Education and Science (1991). *National Curriculum: Interim Report of the Music Working Group*. London: HMSO.

Department of Education for Northern Ireland (1992). *Music: Programmes of Study and Attainment Targets*. London: HMSO.

Dimond, S. J. and Beaumont, J. G. (1974). *Hemisphere Function in the Human Brain*. London: Elek.

Dowling, W. J. and Harwood, D. L. (1986). *Music Cognition*. New York: Academic Press.

Edwards, B. (1979). *Drawing on the Right Side of the Brain*. London: Fontana.

Eisman, L. (1968). *Making Music Your Own*. Morristown, NJ: Silver Burdett.

Ferguson, M. (1973). *The Brain Revolution*. New York: Taplinger.

Gabriel, P. (1994). *Xplora*. Real World CD-Rom.

Gardner, H. et al. (1982). "First intimations of artistry", in S. Strauss and R. Storey (eds), *U-Shaped Behavioral Growth*. New York: Academic Press.

Glover, J. and Ward, S. (1993). *Teaching Music in the Primary School*. London: Cassell.

Hargreaves, D. J. (1986). *The Developmental Psychology of Music*. Cambridge: Cambridge University Press.

Hennesy, S. (1995). *Music 7–11*. London: Routledge.

Hermann, N. (1992). *The Creative Brain*. North Carolina: Hermann Institute.

Hildesheimer, W. (1977). *Mozart*. Frankfurt am Main: Suhrkamp; Eng. trans., 1979.

Jones, G. (1994). *Music of Indonesia: Exploring Music of the World*. London: WOMAD/Heinemann.

Langer, S. (1948). *Philosophy in a New Key*. New York: Mentor.

Levy, J. (1968). "Differential perceptual capacities in major and minor hemispheres", *Proceedings of the National Academy of Science*, 61.

Levy, J. et al. (1972). "Perception of bilateral chimeric figures following hemispheric deconnexion", *Brain*, 95.

Martin, O. S. M. (1982). "Neurological aspects of music perception and performance", in D. Deutsch (ed.), *The Psychology of Music*. New York: Academic Press.

Mellers, W. (1965). *Caliban Reborn*. London: Gollancz.

Meyer, L. B. (1956). *Emotion and Meaning in Music*. Chicago: University of Chicago Press.

Miller, J. R. and Careterette, E. C. (1975). "Perceptual space for musical structures", *Journal of the Acoustical Society of America*, 58, 3.

Mills, J. (1991). *Music in the Primary School*. Cambridge: Cambridge University Press.

Moog, H. (1976). *The Musical Experience of the Pre-School Child*. London: Schott.

Mouncastle, V. (ed.) (1962). *Interhemispheric Relations and Cerebral Dominance*. New York: Johns Hopkins University Press.

O'Connor, J. (1987). *Not Pulling Strings*. London: Lambent.

Ornstein, R. E. (1977). *The Psychology of Consciousness*. 2nd edn, New York: Harcourt Brace.

Paynter, J. (1991). *Sound and Structure*. Cambridge: Cambridge University Press.

Preston, H. (1993). *Listening, Appraising and Composing*. Reading: Berkshire Department of Education.

Regelski, T. (1981). *Teaching General Music*. New York: Schirmer.

Reimer, B. (1989). *A Philosophy of Music Education*. 2nd edn, Englewood Cliffs, NJ: Prentice-Hall.

Reimer, B. and Smith, R. A. (ed.) (1992). *The Arts, Education and Aesthetic Knowing*. Chicago: University of Chicago Press.

Robertson, P. (1992). "The great divide", *BBC Music Magazine*. May.

Sachs, C. (1943). *The Rise of Music in the Ancient World: East and West*. New York: Norton.

Samples, B. (1976). *The Metaphoric Mind*. New York: Addison-Wesley.

Schafer, M. (1963). *British Composers in Interview*. London: Faber & Faber.

Scottish Office (1992). *Expressive Arts 5–14*. London: HMSO.

Sloboda, J. (1985). *The Musical Mind*. Oxford: Oxford University Press.

Sperry, R. W. (1968). "Hemisphere deconnection and unity in conscious awareness", *American Psychologist*, 23.

Sperry, R. W. and Levy, J. (1968). "Differential perceptual capacities in major and minor hemispheres", *Proceedings of the National Academy of Science*, 61.

Stephens, J. and Hanke, M. (1993). *Silver Burdett Planning Guide*. London: Simon & Schuster.

Storr, A. (1992). *Music and the Mind*. London: Harper Collins.

Stowasser, H. (1993). "Some personal observations of music education in Australia, North America and Great Britain", *ISME Journal*, 22.

Swanwick, K. (1979). *A Basis for Music Education*. London: NFER.

Swanwick, K. (1988). *Music, Mind and Education*. London: Routledge.

Swanwick, K. (1994). *Musical Knowledge*. London: Routledge.

Swanwick, K. and Tillman, J. (1986). "The sequence of musical development", *British Journal of Music Education*.

Walker, K. (1957). *Gurdjieff: a Study of his Teaching*. London: Jonathan Cape.

Waters, S. (1994). *Living Without Boundaries*. Bath: BCHE.

Welsh Office (1992). *Music in the National Curriculum (Wales)*. London: HMSO.

Wilson, F. R. (1985). "Music as basic schooling for the brain", *Music Education Journal*. May.

Winnicott, D. W. (1971). *Playing and Reality*. London: Routledge.

Winter, R. (1985). *The Rite of Spring*. Voyager CD Companion.

Wrathall, C. (1992). "Mind over grey matter", *BBC Music Magazine*. November.

Index

Page numbers in bold indicate a main reference to the subject.

octaves   15, 16, 115
"Old Macdonald"   61
ontology   35–6, 47, 57, 124
opera   41, 60, 89, 110
Orff, Carl   25

paintings   82
parents
    and music education   6
    playing in assembly and class   90
    support and help from   52, 91
    and violin teaching   103
part-singing   90, 91
pastiche or imitative writing   29, 56, 70, 71, 72, 73
pattern (musical)   5, 21, 23, 24, 48, 50, 52
percussion instruments   19, 39–40
    improvisation   67
    pitched   25, 38, 40, 43, 67
performing and performers   v, vi, 5, 7–8, 27, 79
    compare and contrast techniques   102
    comparison of performances   94, 96
    inability to perform without notation   26, 27
    left brain   15
    long-term memory   14
    and notation   50–1, 52
    teacher as performer with student   33
pianists, for schools   90
piano lessons   103, 106–7, 108, 115–16
pictographic notation   37, 40, 47
pitch   115
    contour   19, 23
    fixed points of   64, 82
    infant and nursery class   64
    Key Stage (2)   65
    pitch-centre focus   79
    recording of (and notation)   38, 39, 40, 43, 44, 48, 57, 58, 72
    right hemisphere for recognition   11, 16, 54
    secondary school   82
    shapes   50
    and Sol-fa learning   38–9
planning
    importance of   31–2
    of lessons   8, **119**, 128
    for music education in schools   6, 7
    music in secondary school
        assembly   91, 92–3, 99
"play"   110–12
playing by ear   103, 109, 111–12
poetry   6, 41–2, 96, 110, 121
    used by composers   96
polyphony   95
popular music and songs   39, 92
positive attitudes   98
Positron Emission Tomography   15, 16, 18

postgraduates in music   26
posture   13, 33, 103, 118–19, 120, 121–2, 128
practising an instrument   121–2
pregnancy, music heard in the womb   14, 18, 47
primary schools   5, 6, 16, 95, 98
    assembly and collective worship   88–90
    "carpet activity"   65, 74, 78, 80–1, 93–4, 99
    composing   58, 76, 80–1
    learning to play an instrument   23–4
    musical corners   74
    notation   46, 48
    planning work   31–2
    records   78
    teachers   38
problem-solving   77, 102, 112–13, 116, 120
professional musicians   88, 104
psychomotor control, *see* brain
pulse   5, 21, 65, 86

quavers   45

Rauscher, Dr Frances   84
reading music   4, 35, and *see* notation
recorders (instruments)   23, 67, 100
recordings   33, 43, 81
    as aural stimulus   83
    of children's own songs and music   48, 65, 72, 81
    equipment for   124, 126
    importance of good quality
        playback machinery   83, 93, 124
    of lessons   122
records (of progress and work, etc)   65, 78, 81, 127, 128
    for instrumental teaching   121
referential (embodied) meaning   2, 7
rehearsal   27, 108
Reimer, Bennett   vi, 5, 29–30, 33, 34, 94–5
repertoire   91, 105, 118, 119
repetition   19, 51, 67, 72
    in assemblies   99
    in exploring sound   61
    of listening to music   20, 24, 30, 91, 92, 94
    of movement   14, 21–2
    of scales and arpeggios   107
    for storage in memory   14, 33
reviewing music   96
rhythm   39, 40, 44, 56, 57, 58, 68, 72, 82
    inverted pattern   100
    rhythmic patterns   61, 83
rhythmic (mensural) notation   58
rote-learning   20, 32, 45